HOW *not* TO KILL

your spouse, kids, and coworkers

Dr. Nealy Brown

Sarah Tierney & Shannon Hunt

outskirtspress

DENVER, COLORADO

Outskirts Press, Inc.
http://www.outskirtspress.com

ISBN: 978-1-4787-0904-6

Library of Congress Control Number: 2013912907

Outskirts Press and the "OP" logo are trademarks belonging to Outskirts Press, Inc.

PRINTED IN THE UNITED STATES OF AMERICA

*This book is dedicated to the brave men and women
who choose to create amazing relationships
even with those who are different or difficult.*

Contents

Acknowledgements

Nealy Brown

To the world's greatest husband, whose love, kindness, and maturity enable me to learn how to love people well.

To my daughter, Joy, who demonstrates kindness to everyone she meets.

To my Zack, whose heart of gold and resiliency inspire me.

To my parents, who modeled and equipped me with a spirit of hard work, thick skin, a love of learning, and compassion for the underdog.

To God, who I continue to try to grasp and whose inspired words forever change my life.

To the countless souls who have taught me in our journey together.

Sarah Tierney

To my Jake and my Gwen. My cup runneth over.

To my family and friends. Thank you for your patience with me.

To my dad, Mike Nichols, and to our copy-editor, Emily Hinkel. Thanks for helping us say it best.

To Dr. Brown, for the hurricane force of love and wisdom you are in my life.

To God, for teaching me "the most excellent way."

Shannon Hunt

To my husband, Jeff, you bless me beyond belief. I love our marriage, our friendship, our partnership in life. Thank you for loving me in the good days and bad. Forever Falling!

To Cassidy and Caden, the best kiddos ever! I am so proud of both of you! I love you more, doubter chowder, whatever scever!

To Dad, Mom, Kim, thank you for showing me what true family is. Faith, love . . . and fun!

To Nealy, you sharpen and challenge me. *Thank you* for your friendship and your mentorship.

To God, I am forever grateful for your grace and forgiveness. You are most important.

Preface

For years now, those I've served have asked for a book to remind them of principles that are simple but not always easy to remember and follow. We are happy to offer this humble composition. Nothing in here is new. Nothing is rocket science. Nothing will magically make all your relationships perfect. However, what we can offer you are moments to make you laugh, to make you think, and to challenge you to find ways to have great relationships, even with those who can be difficult. *Many who have learned these principles have found they were able to make amazing relationships where they had never before thought it was possible.*

This book is written for the average Joe. It will encourage you to be creative, to think outside the box, to find out how to make relationships work, and to not give up until you do. Many relationships that seem beyond repair or impossible to improve have had breakthroughs. However, we do not mean to imply that every relationship is worth saving or that you should press on in certain situations, such as when severe domestic violence wreaks havoc on a home or when children are being sexually abused. There are circumstances where the wisest and most loving thing to do in the relationship is to end it. But we believe these cases are few and far between. We have journeyed with many people who felt their only hope was to end the relationship but learned another way. There are times when we feel like giving up or are tempted to believe that the other person is awful, when really they are just different, or perhaps we have not learned how to handle certain human dynamics effectively. Your feelings are not good indicators that a relationship is impossible or that it should end.

Imagine you purchase a new entertainment center that comes neatly shipped in a flat box. You open it up but don't find any instructions or tools. Building the entertainment center you had hoped for would be quite difficult. You may have been excited about the prospect, anticipating how wonderful this new furniture would look in your home. But, low and behold, all you have is a pile of wood. It's not at all what you were hoping for. Now you have a choice. You could return it and look for another one. Or you could find some instructions and tools and learn how to assemble it. It really is a beautiful piece of furniture that you could enjoy for a lifetime. But it will take a little effort on your part to assemble. On the other hand, if you returned it and ordered another, chances are it would come in the same flat box, another seemingly useless pile of wood. Most are going to require some assembly.

Relationships are the same. We tend to want to "return to sender" because we feel we have a defective piece, when really we are just lacking some instructions and tools. It is our hope that these pages offer you the instructions you need and some tools to help you build an amazing relationship with almost anyone. At first, some of the ideas may seem a little off-kilter—or even impossible—just like when you read those assembly instructions and it tells you something about connecting A to B using F, H, and J. It doesn't always make sense at first. But if you will pick up the pieces and give it a try, you may be surprised at what a beautiful relationship you can build.

The ideas within this book have come from my interactions with those I have served. While journeying with brave people who face difficult situations, I've had conversations that have brought to life analogies, illustrations, and acronyms that have helped others deal with the challenges of relationships. The ones you find here are the ones I've compiled because students in my classes, clients in my office, or people who've attended my seminars have said these were key in helping them.

The stories within these pages are true. Sometimes they are detailed facts of actual situations. Other times they are stories we've heard a hundred times from a hundred clients that we have summarized. Where there are cold hard facts, we have received permissions but have sometimes changed the names and any information that might give away their identities. The summaries are just as true because they seem to represent a theme in human relationships.

I have been blessed to receive help from fellow professionals in putting this together. In case you are curious, whenever you see "I," it refers to Nealy Brown. Wherever Shannon Hunt or Sarah Tierney share a story, their name will be mentioned. Shannon and Sarah have helped craft, reword, and explain these ideas more effectively. Sarah has helped with the brunt of the editing, taking piles of transcripts, notes, emails, and recordings to make the body of this book. Shannon has helped to edit and bring the material home by providing ideas for application. Together we hope it speaks to your heart and strengthens your resolve.

We're not sure what it is that you are facing right now that led you to pick up this book. My guess is that you are hoping to make something better. You may even feel frustrated or hopeless. Perhaps your work or home is becoming almost unbearable. Hang in there because we might just have some answers, a rope to pull you out of the rut you've been in.

This book is for us, too. See, these principles are simple but not easy. They are principles that we need to be constantly reminded of because of our human side. It is so easy to forget and get frustrated with our spouses, kids, and coworkers. You may find that you read this book every year—or maybe even every month—until these ideas become habits. It may end up becoming part of your bathroom décor, in order to find a few minutes each day to refocus and be reminded how to find joy in situations that upset you. Whatever your process may be, we applaud you because you care enough to find new ways to make life better for yourself and others. We hope you find that in these pages.

Silence is Golden
Learning when we don't need to talk about it

> *"Remember not only to say the right thing in the right place, but far more difficult still, to leave unsaid the wrong thing at the tempting moment."*
> Benjamin Franklin

I am often asked by newly married wives, "How do I get my husband to get me the gift that I want?" My response: "You send him the link on the Internet and say 'Buy this.'"

But I make it simpler still. I buy the gift myself and then tell my husband, "Look what you got me!" And he smiles and says, "Am I going to wrap it?" And I say, "No, because I'm using it now. You can wrap it the day before Christmas, but until then, I'm using it." We've been married almost fifteen years, and I now text him when we're going on a date. He texts back, "Am I bringing you flowers?" And I say, "No, you're bringing me chocolate." It's a very simple process. It's not Hollywood romance, but it works marvelously for us.

So naturally, I was very surprised and impressed when he told me he was taking me out on a date. My idea of a good date is romantic: I want cloth napkins and low lights. Men don't automatically understand your idea of romantic, by the way. We all interpret words differently, and my husband speaks engineer, so he has needed some translation in this area.

He informed me that this was not a romantic date, so that I would not be disappointed, but assured me that it was a "fun date." I'm thinking we're going boating—this would be my definition of a fun date—but instead we begin driving through Atlanta rush hour traffic. The reason I live on the south side of Atlanta is because I hate rush hour traffic and want to avoid it at all costs. My husband, on the other hand, believes he is Mario Andretti, and the distance between our car and the car in front of us can usually be calculated in centimeters. This is very difficult for me, but I make it through the traffic, and we arrive at our destination: a Brad Paisley concert.

The problem is that I hate concerts. While I think Brad Paisley is a lyrical genius, I hate noise, I hate crowds, and I hate sitting for hours and hours. I am an introvert; I prefer to work at home, in my own little cubby hole, where there is peace and quiet and no other human beings. I'm thinking,

"We've been married years. Have I ever asked to go to a concert? No. And when you tell me you're going to a concert, I don't go, because I don't want to go."

But now we're at this concert and I'm doing everything I can to keep a poker face. Why? Because I believe this is the most loving thing to do in this moment. This is the question I wish I would ask myself in every situation: "What is the most loving and wise thing to do?" And this time, I determine that the most loving thing to do is for me to be an appreciative wife, keep my mouth shut and try my best to look happy because this man has so thoughtfully and lovingly planned this date for me.

So I sit there for what feels to me like ten hours, and I don't say anything. This is a *huge* accomplishment for me—one of few times in my life when I have succeeded in keeping my mouth shut. But if I were to have said, "Really, a concert?! Please don't do this to me again," even if I had used the most loving words, do you think he'd ever plan a date again? (And this, by the way, is why men don't make romantic gestures for us, because they feel so incompetent: they burn the dinner, they forget the candlelight, they don't provide the most stimulating conversation.) Even if we feel horribly disappointed, when someone offers us a loving gesture, our best response is to give them the gift of graciousness in return.

If your mother raised you well, what do you do when someone gives you a gift? You say, "Thank you." No matter how ugly or cheap it is. When your children bring you macaroni necklaces, how do you respond? You are thankful. Why? Because you see the love behind the gift and not the glue that gets all over your shirt. The other people in your life are just overgrown children, and when they bring you those imperfect macaroni necklaces, you must graciously and thankfully receive them. While the old adage, "If you don't have anything nice to say, don't say anything at all," is certainly true, I prefer to think that there is always something nice that can be said: at the very least, "thank you."

I have a friend, Mary, who sometimes visits our family and stays for the weekend. This weekend, Mary brought a cooler of food to our house. Now, I'm usually known for being a rather good hostess. Though I don't cook all that well, I definitely make provisions for company. Mary is on a special diet that requires her to eat a particularly pricey cut of steak, and knowing this, I typically go to the grocery store and buy her all the special food she needs, including the steak. However, this time when I called to find out what and how much to buy, Mary told me she did not want to inconvenience me and was bringing it all herself. I found this odd, since I have always bought groceries and she has had no qualms about listing out exactly what she wants, making specific requests right down to the brand. But I think I know what was happening this time...

I think I can say with 90% certainty that Mary does not like the quality of food I buy. You see, Mary ended up doing quite well for herself in life, and she enjoys a certain level of luxury. She only buys her meat from one particular butcher in town who specializes in beef. I have seen her nonverbal reactions on previous visits, when looking over the cut of meat or the vegetables. Mary was polite; she didn't say a word and ate every bite. But it was evident to me that the food did not meet her standards. So this time, she simply decided to meet these standards herself, without making a request of me and without condemning our lack of quality grocery stores or my inexperience at choosing quality meat. Mary kept her mouth shut and, instead, took action.

When I ponder this scenario, I think of how many ways her actions could have been interpreted. I could have been royally offended. How insulting to believe that my food was substandard! I could have taken offense at a guest arriving for dinner with groceries, thinking to themselves, "She thinks we can't take care of it!?" It's interesting, the stories we write.

In this case, I chose to be grateful. I do not want to spend the amount it costs for Mary's standard of food, and I was grateful she did not ask me. Though I would never spend that much on groceries in a month for my family, I would have spent that much on a few days of groceries for her. But I'm so glad she did not ask me and even more glad that we didn't talk about it.

Silence is often such a special gift. Sure, sometimes addressing the elephant in the room relieves tension and creates peace, but I'm reminded more and more how silence is golden. I enjoyed a wonderful weekend with Mary. We enjoyed her company, she enjoyed her steaks, and I enjoyed not having to pay for them. What a gift it can be to *not* talk about it and simply adjust accordingly.

This is a simple idea but certainly not easy. Furthermore, it can go against every fiber of our being. Our society has taught us we should share our feelings and tell others when they hurt us. Most people would even say that they want you to share these things with them. Sometimes sharing *is* helpful; if issues come up over and over again, and we are truly invested in creating a win-win solution, sharing can be a useful tool. However, with some practice, I've come to believe that *not* sharing can be a great gift that relieves us all of quite a lot of unnecessary withdrawals from our relationship. Frankly, this has taken me years to be convinced of and to be able to implement. It can be very, *very* difficult to stay silent when we have been taught otherwise for so long. That age old adage of "If you don't have something nice to say, don't say it at all" got lost somewhere along the way, and we are paying for it in our relationships.

One trick that has helped me to stay silent is to implement the "30 day rule" in which I would ask myself a month later whether or not the issue really needed to be brought up. Frankly, I cannot think of *a single thing* I decided was worth bringing up. It's important to set a specific date; otherwise, we encounter those moments of annoyance as they arise and decide, "See, I'm upset, I should tell him," when really we're just irritated in the moment and we can get over it. If we would wait, we would see that it really isn't as significant as it seemed in the moment.

I say all this with one caveat: we have to stay engaged in the relationship. Sometimes when we don't address things, we still feel uncomfortable about it and it shows. We intentionally or unintentionally avoid the other person or reduce our interactions with them because we feel awkward or angry. **What I'm suggesting is that we stay silent on the issue but stay engaged in the relationship.** This is exactly what Mary did. She did not allow the steak to come between us, nor did she make an issue out of it. She didn't start avoiding my house; she bought her groceries, and she still stayed engaged in our friendship.

> *What I'm suggesting is that we stay silent on the issue but stay engaged in the relationship.*

There are other times when a subject needs a rest or becomes off limits for a season. In those situations, we can choose silence or change the subject because that conversation doesn't go well for anyone. I have a friend, Carmen, who asked her family to keep their comments to themselves regarding her spouse. They were very critical of him, and their opinions were not helpful. At first, Carmen avoided her family altogether because of their continued criticism. But she then learned to just change the subject when it came to him. After that, she readily contacted them and shared other areas of her life, such as work, school, and the kids. We can always converse on a lot of other topics and intentionally reach out with kindness and love to stay engaged in the relationship.

At times there are long term problems that are better resolved if we lay them out plainly and work toward a win-win solution with the other person, which we talk about elsewhere in this book. However, for many things, we can act on our own to make the situation better without ever bringing it up. **I think our first solution, and often the only solution we need, is to have the policy: "Silence is golden, but stay engaged."**

HOW TO APPLY THIS TO YOUR LIFE:

Think of a time when you have chosen to talk about it or point it out when you could have given the gift of silence instead. **Who are the people in your life who could use the gift of silence from you more often?**

Think of current situations where it would be wise to practice "silence is golden" and just take care of it yourself, like Mary did with her quality steaks.

Think of current situation or situations where it would be wise to practice "silence is golden." **In each case, how can you stay engaged even while remaining silent about something,** like Carmen did?

2

Plan B, C, . . .or Z!
If I want it, I'm responsible for it.

"The key to success is the ability to go from one failure to the next with no loss of enthusiasm." Winston Churchill

I have two separate chairs in my counseling office that tend to give me a great indication of where a couple stands in their relationship. For instance, during premarital counseling, they move the chairs as close together as possible. But during one particular marital counseling session, when the couple came into my office, the wife immediately picked up her chair and moved it over to the opposite wall. Their relationship was a complete mess; they had not been sleeping in the same room for two years, and she was only staying so that he could continue to take care of her bills.

A week later I was called by the Air Force and found out I would be traveling overseas to serve for two months. I wasn't sure this couple would make it another two months, and I only had one more session left with them before I left (and I would likely be unreachable during my time away). So I told them to bring their calendar and a list of four babysitters, and we sat down and scheduled a date night every week for the next eight weeks. Because they didn't have much money for restaurants or shows, they decided to feed the ducks at the lake and buy dollar ice cream cones.

When I returned home eight weeks later, I was naturally very anxious to see if their relationship had already ended, but they scheduled an appointment with me. The wife again grabbed the chair...but this time she pushed it over next to her husband, sat down, and started rubbing her foot up and down the back of his leg! This is a great reminder to me of how simple relationships can be, because after only eight weeks of date night, progress was being made rather quickly! Before, they had not slept in the same room for two years. She loathed his very presence. All they needed was to start having some fun together and to reconnect with one another, but with work and kids and schedules, there had been no opportunities for this. Eight weeks of date night began to turn things around.

This is not rocket science. Sometimes it really is this simple. I've seen it many, many times. When we focus solely on having a good time together, everything else gets put on the back burner and our problems are off-limits for discussion. The key is to increase deposits to the love tank while decreasing withdrawals. Moments like date night are specifically set aside to increase those deposits. At work, we celebrate birthdays and give bonuses. At home with our kids, we have game night or we might share the top three highlights of our day at dinner. And for marriages, we have date night.

But what if the other person is never around so that you can connect? This was the problem of one wife who came in and told me that her husband was a workaholic. He was a big executive in the company and worked all the time. Quality time was extremely important to her, but she could not cajole this man into committing to a date night.

She told me, "I've tried everything!" and I said, "Well, tell what you've tried, because it's helpful to know both what works and what does not work." So she listed off all the many occasions that she had asked him, at different times and in different ways (because it's not only important *what* you say and *how* you say it, but also *when* you say it). After we made a long list, I turned to her and said, "You've only tried one thing." I actually thought she might smack me: "What do you mean I've only tried one thing?!"

I said, "You've tried this one thing in a lot of really creative ways…but it seems to me that all you've ever done is talk about it with him. Sounds like talking doesn't work."

No matter how she tried to have that conversation—and she had devised a number of creative, kind, and respectful ways to have it—he still would not commit. Plan A had failed, so we devised Plan B…

Because he's a workaholic, he had a computer at home and a computer at work. She went into the calendar on his home computer and noticed that whenever he met with a new client, he simply put "meeting" along with the location. So she began to schedule "meetings" for them. The first time, she entered, "Meeting, 7 o'clock, Texas Roadhouse." That evening, he called home to let her know he'd be late because he "had a meeting." When he approached their table at 7:00, he was naturally quite surprised to see her there. She smiled and said, "We've got a meeting—it's on the calendar."

He was a little miffed and scolded her for her scheme, though they ended up having a good time. But she continued to use this method—scheduling dates as "Meeting, 5 o'clock, Panera Bread"—and they continued having a wonderful time! What she wanted was a worthy goal, good for both parties involved (this is the difference between being manipulative and being creative, by the way), and her perseverance in using her imagination solved a big problem. After some time, he no longer scolded her, but thanked her.

He could have reworked the way he scheduled meetings so that it was apparent whether or not it was his wife. He could have failed to show up. But he didn't. If he had, I hope she would have moved on to Plan C. It would be easy to get discouraged and give up, but giving up hurts us all. If we are smart, we'll get over our pity parties and move forward to the next plan.

One of my friends had a similar problem with her boss. She had work that required his input in order for her to accomplish it. She sent emails and left voicemails, but he was terrible about responding. She often had a list of questions or issues that only he could address. After much trial and error, she discovered that he always went to his office after his weekly Thursday meeting, even if just for a moment. She had tried to schedule this time with him but to no avail. Finally, she learned that if she was waiting by his doorway on Thursdays after his meeting with her list of questions in hand, she could quickly rattle them off and get the answers she needed to proceed.

What do you want in your relationships? Think about what you want, not about what you don't want. We set out to fail when we start focusing on the problem, saying, "You shouldn't do this and you shouldn't do that." Think about what it is you really, *specifically* want. We set out to fail when we make generic requests such as "I wish you would be more romantic" or "You need to get off my back." How, exactly, do you get off someone's back? Think in terms of actions—if he were being more romantic, what kinds of things would he be doing? If she were off your back, how would you know?

God bless my college roommates; they had a lot of wonderful attributes, but one thing they were *not* is neat. They liked to be comfortable and have a "lived in" house: magazines by the couch, books on the coffee table, mail on the dining room table. It was cluttered, and I don't like clutter. Now that I have my own house, when people come to visit they often remark, "Oh, you haven't unpacked yet?" That is literally how bare my house is.

Due to those years spent with messy roommates, I now have "dining room table issues." I once had a friend living with me, and when she moved in, I informed her, "If you put anything on my dining room table, I will throw it off the balcony" (and she knew me well enough to know I was completely serious). Yes, it's true: I have dining room table issues. I won't even put a centerpiece on the dining room table because then there's something *on* it.

When I was first married, my husband would come home and empty his pockets all over my dining room table. There would be keys, a wallet, receipts, and a monstrosity of coins on my table. Somehow sanity prevailed, and I kindly said to my sweet new husband, "Would you please put your keys and other things somewhere else?" And he would try, but day after day he would forget, and I would again find his pocket contents *on my table!*

So I came up with a plan. In our house, when you enter from the garage, you pass through the laundry room, so I asked, "Sweetheart, could you please put your keys on the dryer?" And of course, the good-hearted guy that he is, he said, "Absolutely, honey, I'll put 'em on the dryer, no problem!" So the next day, he walked through the laundry room…and went right to the dining room table, as if it were a giant magnet, and unloaded his pockets. He was not trying to be malicious or unkind. He was not lying when he said he planned to put his things on the dryer. He just doesn't have dining room table issues, so he doesn't think about or desire an empty dining room table.

So then I tried Plan B. I put a cabinet right next to the door inside the garage, so he would see it when he pulled in. He happily agreed to unload his pockets here instead. I was being creative. **You can have what you want in life; you just have to find a creative solution.** Unfortunately, he went straight for my dining room table yet again out of habit, forgetting our agreement.

You can have what you want in life; you just have to find a creative solution.

He said to me, "I pull into the garage, I get my keys out, and I immediately think to myself, 'Keys do not belong on the dining room table; they belong somewhere else' (probably because he's heard that from me a hundred times), but the problem is that by the time I get to the door, I lose the thought." So I then decided, "I'm going to make something! Yes, some kind of sign, and I'll put it outside, right by the door in the garage so it will remind him—and this time, it's going to work!" No, it didn't work. It wasn't for lack of creative thinking on my end and certainly not for a lack of care on his part, because he was probably more frustrated than I was at this point. After all, he didn't even have a problem before I gave him one! And so now we *both* have this problem, and nothing is working…

Marriage has taught me many things. When we were first married, my husband was crazy about Corvettes. He would always point them out—"Did you see that Corvette?" "No, honey, I did not see the Corvette." I never see the Corvette. It's not that they're invisible, but I don't notice Corvettes because I'm not the one madly in love with Corvettes. Fifteen years later, I might occasionally see a Corvette because he has pointed them out so many times—but, even now, it's rare.

Many people have these kinds of "visual impairments." How can someone be so blind to something that is so apparent to me? It's **because we notice what we value.** For a while, I did not understand why my husband, though perfectly willing, was unable to accomplish the very simple task of keeping the dining room table empty. But now I know the reason. It's not a Corvette—it doesn't matter to him. If I had said, "Please put your keys and wallet in the bedroom, and then I'll buy you a Corvette," I bet he'd have gotten those keys off the dining room table! It wasn't a matter of not wanting to or not being able to, my husband just doesn't notice it. He doesn't value it the same way I do. *I'm* the one with the dining room table issues, not him. How many conflicts are we having over the keys on the dining room table? How much damage are we doing to our relationship because of the keys on the dining room table?

> *Many people have these kinds of "visual impairments." ...because we notice what we value.*

Some arguments stem from the fact that I wanted you to do something for me or treat me in a certain way because I feel like I need you to make me happy. For example, I might want you to spend more time with me. This is a good want; there's nothing wrong with this want. But when this want goes unmet, I can still recognize that I don't need *you* to fill me up and make me feel happy. I can look for all sorts of ways to do that on my own; I have hundreds of options before me. I don't *need* to have you make me happy. I can actually do that myself. If I'm smart, I'll find creative ways to spend time with you. Unfortunately, I might be hurt or upset because I'm looking to you to do a certain thing or act a certain way; when you don't, I sit over here and live in my sadness, instead of being smart and looking for other ways to be fulfilled in life. For instance, I wanted you to take me to that special place on my birthday, and you didn't. I just wanted dinner done and the house clean, and it wasn't. These moments eat at us and rob us of our joy.

What I finally did, after my husband emptied his keys and wallet and receipts and quarters all over my dining room table day after day, was… drumroll please…to pick them up and put them in the other room. Every day he'd unload, and every day I would scoop his things into a bowl and put them in the other room. It took maybe five seconds to move them.

If I want the keys to be somewhere else, why don't I put the keys somewhere else? **If I want it, then I'm the one responsible for it.** As crazy and simple as that sounds, it's incredibly helpful. How many arguments happen in our relationships because I'm focusing on *you* changing? You'd be surprised what you can do for yourself. If you're the one who wants the laundry off the floor, then pick it up. If you're the one who wants to save money on the electric bill, then turn the lights off. If you're the one who wants a romantic date, then plan an evening. If you want the house clean, either clean it or hire a housekeeper. How many arguments are we having about the lights or the laundry or whatever it may be for you? If you want it, you're responsible for it.

> *If I want it, then I'm the one responsible for it.*

HOW TO APPLY THIS TO YOUR LIFE:

What is your dining room table dilemma? What request has your spouse, child, or coworker seemingly ignored? Is it the messy cubicle that you requested be tidied? Is it the stereo that's constantly on in the garage even after you asked him a million times to turn it off? Or maybe you have an unspoken expectation: "She should know that I need at least a half hour at home after work before being bombarded with stuff about the kids." **What is that request or expectation that is not being met?**

This is something that *you* value, and it may not be something your spouse, child, or coworker values. And that's okay. So, if this is something that *you* value and something that *you* want, how will you get what you want? **Write down three different strategies to get what you want**, keeping in mind that you can't change the other person.

3

Trash the Trivial
Living our priorities

> *"You have to decide what your highest priorities are and have the courage—
> pleasantly, smilingly, unapologetically, to say 'no' to other things. And the way
> you do that is by having a bigger 'yes' burning inside. The enemy of the 'best'
> is often the 'good.' The main thing is to keep the main thing the main thing."*
> Stephen R. Covey

It was around Thanksgiving when Julie was diagnosed with leukemia, and soon after, they took her bone marrow to find a donor. She was twenty-eight years old at the time. She and my brother had been married just a few years and had two precious boys, ages three and one. Over Christmas the whole family became acquainted with leukemia, the process for healing and recovery, and the wait to find a donor. Luckily, it was not a quick-spreading disease, so even though the wait for a donor might be months, she had time.

Then, in January 2003, the news came. Only a few months after her diagnosis, we found out that she had a very rare genetic makeup, and finding a donor was highly unlikely. Not only were there none in the donor database, but with her DNA, there was almost zero chance that anyone would ever match. We began to mourn. We began to seek answers to the many "why" questions that come at times like this. Why her? Why so young? Why leave two precious little boys without a mother? Why no donor? Why?!

The months passed, and we enjoyed our time together. The family photo we had taken that Christmas took on new meaning: it might be her last Christmas. Watching the boys laugh and play, oblivious to what they would have to suffer at their young ages, we could no longer laugh with them. It was a solemn time as we waited for her to die.

My time with her would be even shorter. Because I was beginning my service as a chaplain in the Air Force, I had two upcoming military trainings. So I found myself in Alabama at Maxwell Air Force Base making frequent calls home. It seemed odd to me how much Julie asked how I was doing and how often she would encourage me. Things continued this way for a while until one day, the call came.

By some unbelievable chance, a donor had been found! I still remember the tears of joy that fell as I heard the news. It was a miracle! The whirlwind began as appointments were made, and my family wore out the interstate between St. Louis and their small town in southern Illinois. By May, she had her bone marrow transplant and everything was going well. We could not have been happier! I made calls yet again from my chaplain training during that steamy July in Alabama, and I heard good news followed by more good news. Her body had accepted the bone marrow, and her anti-rejection medicine was working. It would not be long before she would be able to come home!

Finally, the scheduled day was only a couple weeks away; she was finally going to be home and all was well. I returned to base after a long drive from Alabama and served a few days before I was to head home. I was at Grissom Air Force Base at the time, a rather desolate place with no cell phone reception. When I finally headed home, it was about an hour before I was able to get cell phone service and could check my voicemail. I had about a dozen messages. One by one, I listened to each call that had occurred over the last few days. In a matter of minutes, I heard the entire story unfold, beginning with a concerned but hopeful message that Julie had had some complications, until I reached the final tear-filled message telling me that Julie had died.

Nothing can explain the pain you feel in those moments. I have lost many people in my life. We had a large family, so I was accustomed to funerals from a young age, even funerals for those who were young themselves. But nothing prepared me for the devastating grief I now faced and the anger I felt toward God.

Luckily for Julie, she had lived in such a way that she had no regrets. She worked at home as a medical transcriptionist, while my brother worked as a chemist in a lab he had set up at home. They had pursued what was most important to them—their family. They both got to stay home with the boys and with each other. They lived their priorities.

During this time, I realized that I had not. I worked myself to the bone, spending too much time doing things that didn't matter. I didn't want to be on my death bed, having let life pass me by while all I did was work. I vowed to restructure my life and focus my priorities on the people who mattered to me. And that's what I did.

Julie was not my only example of a life lived with no regrets. My best friend, Jennifer, followed suit. When she had kids, she stopped working to stay at home and, eventually, home school her kids. She was tireless in her efforts to provide her children with the best values and the best education. Her husband was a contractor, so they often got to spend time with him on job sites when they finished their schoolwork. He even landed a contract in Hawaii, and they went there to live for a few months while he built. Jennifer was living it up, teaching her children under the warm Hawaiian sun and enjoying the beauty of nature each afternoon. They were almost done with the building project and were making plans to come back to Colorado when her two boys were caught in an undertow in the ocean. She was able to save one of them, but the other was swept out to sea, and a few hours later, comatose from her near drowning, Jennifer died.

Only two years later, I found myself, once again, evaluating my life. And, once again, I found myself coming up short. I had so wholeheartedly committed to living out what mattered only two years earlier. Yet here I was, still spinning my tires and spending so much time on things that really didn't matter. So I sat down and made a list of the unimportant tasks in my life, so that I would have a clear guide to keep me focused on what did matter. I made my list and made my plan of action. I wasn't going to waste any more of my life.

In his bestseller, *First Things First*, Stephen R. Covey[1] says that we spend time in one of four ways. He developed a simple matrix dividing tasks into "urgent" and "not urgent," along with "important" and "unimportant." He concludes that 90% of human activity tends to be in the "urgent unimportant" category. In other words, 90% of what we do is what is calling for our attention in the moment but is really not important, like a ringing phone or an interruption by a coworker at our cubical. He says our days get consumed by what is pressing on us in the moment rather than what really matters.

In the spirit of living only by what was important, I used only paper plates and plastic forks for years (it's not as expensive as you might think with mass ordering from Amazon). This is still mainly what I use. For years, I cooked only microwave meals and frozen pizzas (my spouse and kids didn't really care—they'll eat whatever you put in front of them). I didn't want precious time to be wasted on laundry and cooking. My husband wears undershirts every day because he's a big, sweaty guy, and one day I realized that I was spending too much time folding these undershirts. I thought, "Why do I fold this? No one even *sees* it! Why have I spent all these years folding t-shirts no one even sees!?" So my husband now has a basket of undershirts, and he just grabs one in the morning—no folding required. Anything that is not worn on the outside or is not worn outside the house does not get folded or hung or even put away. I have *nine* laundry baskets. They cost $3 each. So for $27, I get back hours upon hours of my life by not folding, not matching socks, not putting away underclothes, etc. I'm convinced **we're all so busy manicuring our lawns and folding our underwear that we're missing out on the really important stuff in life**. For some people, nutrition or finances or cleaning

> *...we're all so busy manicuring our lawns and folding our underwear that we're missing out on the really important stuff in life.*

or gardening or cooking are a priority or a passion, but for me, my time with my family is my top priority and passion; most everything else is unimportant. You can choose your own values, but whatever values you choose, you must let them drive your life, instead of what's pressing in the moment or what's important to someone else.

Sure, there are things that need to be done, and some of those things are rather mundane. But we can make an impact by ensuring we are not making our spouses, kids, and coworkers busy with unimportant tasks. My boss was so helpful to me when, each year in our annual meeting, he had us write up everything we were doing, cross off the unimportant tasks, and prioritize the important ones. When things are swamped at work, I'm often amazed at how many items there are on my to-do list that don't get done, and yet no one ever asks about them again!

Likewise, there's value in teaching our kids responsibility, but there are *lots* of areas to do that, and lots of areas that *really don't matter*. As much as it killed me, when my kids were teenagers, I would not let the cleanliness of their rooms become a battle between us. My son really put me to the test on this one—and yes, I did regularly spray his room for bugs—but I continued to remind myself that clean rooms do not matter. Why? Because over time, the fights we have about the cleanliness of the room can suck all the love out of that heart and kill the relationship. And the relationship is more important than the clean room. The relationship is more important than the laundry. The relationship is even more important than being right. The relationship is more important. We must not miss out on what really matters.

If you knew you were going to die in one year, what would you do? If you knew you were going to die in one month, what would you do? Whatever your priorities are, don't get caught up doing the trivial things and missing what really matters. **At the end of your life, you will not be regretting all the clothes you didn't fold or all the weeds you didn't pull. You will be regretting all the things you did not say or do in your relationships.** For most of us, relationships are more important.

> *At the end of your life, you will not be regretting all the clothes you didn't fold or all the weeds you didn't pull. You will be regretting all the things you did not say or do in your relationships.*

HOW TO APPLY THIS TO YOUR LIFE:

I know it may drive you nuts that the dishes are in the sink, that the files are unorganized, or that your daughter wants pink hair and piercings. (Breathe.) Those things really don't matter. You may even need to repeat this to yourself: "Those things really don't matter." Your relationships matter. It's time to be real with yourself. **What have you made a priority that's actually unimportant?** (If you're like me, there are probably several things. Write them all down!)

What is truly important to you?

While you've been focusing on the unimportant, what have you been sacrificing? **What have you missed out on that is important because you were spending too much time on the unimportant?**

Further reading:
   Covey, Stephen R. *First Things First.* New York: Simon and Shuster, 2001.
   Covey, Stephen R. *The 7 Habits of Highly Effective People.* New York: Simon and Shuster, 2003.

4

Plugging the Leaks
Stopping the downward spiral of emotion

"When another person makes you suffer, it is because he suffers deeply within himself, and his suffering is spilling over. He does not need punishment; he needs help. That's the message he is sending." Thich Naht Hanh

Loud clanging filled the shop as he knocked the tools from the shelf with one swoop of his arm. The mechanics in the shop stood in stunned silence as their manager, Mark, stormed back into his office, slamming the door behind him. Then it started. A small circle formed as a few mechanics began their diatribe: "He always overreacts!" and "What an #@%hole!" This went on until their work started piling up again.

These mechanics would go home in a bad mood, just as mad as Mark had been that morning. Some would take it out on the drivers on the road, others on their families, and many would repeat that morning's events over and over. But the one who felt it the most was Dan. The nine-digit item numbers had been off by only one number. Anyone could have mixed up the parts, but this mistake cost them $750. He was tired of Mark's temper. He was done with this place.

Emotion travels rapidly. You can see it easily in a room full of toddlers. If one starts crying, others will soon begin crying too. It's a shame we don't outgrow it. We have to work hard to overcome this natural reaction, but it's worth the work in the end. You see, Dan left his job for another. It paid less and offered fewer benefits, but he said he was happier. And he was, until his new manager got angry too.

We could take sides, and most of us will. Some of us side with Dan. After all, who wants to work in a hostile environment? Others side with Mark. Who wouldn't be upset over a $750 loss? And we'd be right. It would be reasonable to side with either of them. No one really likes angry outbursts, and no one likes losing money either. Both seem to be reasonable responses. In fact, this is usually the case. **Most of the time, if we stopped to think about it, we would agree that people's**

> *Most of the time, if we stopped to think about it, we would agree that people's emotional responses are actually reasonable.*

emotional responses are actually reasonable. We may or may not have the same response ourselves, but many reasonable people would have. Moreover, most of us get emotional, even over little things, when we are under stress. In some cases, someone might be reasonably upset simply because of the pressure they are under. We all get emotional at times.

Think about the last time someone you know was upset. Maybe your teenage daughter cried as she got ready for homecoming. But don't we all want to look our best? Maybe your spouse gave you the silent treatment because you forgot to fix the dishwasher—again! Haven't you ever been upset by someone's forgetfulness? Maybe your boss got blindsided in the meeting, not expecting the loss of sales to be so great. Who hasn't been upset over losing money or the possibility of losing a job?

People are going to get upset. Whether we yell, cry, walk away, or throw tools on the shop floor, we all get upset. We are all leaking emotion. **The problem is that we allow other people's emotion to leak onto us.** The emotion travels through the room and leaks all over us. **Then we leak all over others, and the chain reaction begins.** It impacts how we respond to the person who is demonstrating emotion, how we treat others, how we do or don't do our tasks afterward, etc. The impact can be devastating, like a flood destroying everything in its path. This is a normal process of life—a normal one, but not a good one.

> *The problem is that we allow other people's emotion to leak onto us. Then we leak all over others, and the chain reaction begins.*

What if, after the rainstorm of emotion hits, we pause for a moment to dry off? What if we refuse to allow the emotional spill to leak onto us? What if we plugged the leak? And if, once we plugged the leak, it only poured out another crack, what if we tried again? What if we kept it from leaking onto others as well? Could we end this madness? Most of the time, I'm guessing we could.

Imagine that the scenario above had a different ending. Loud clanging filled the shop as he knocked the tools from the shelf with one swoop of his arm. The mechanics in the shop stood in stunned silence as their manager, Mark, stormed back into his office, slamming the door behind him. Then it started. A small circle formed as a few mechanics began their diatribe: "He always overreacts!" and "What an #@%hole!" Frank took a deep breath and regrouped. After a minute, he chimed in, "Mark sure didn't handle that well, but I'd hate to be in his shoes and have to answer for that $750. He'll get over it soon enough." Then Frank changed the subject to the college basketball championship. It didn't take long before everyone was laughing again!

Frank's tactics were quite effective. He changed his own negative thoughts about the situation and allowed Mark to be upset *without being upset in return*. He didn't defend Mark's response, but he helped the group see Mark's side of the situation. He changed the subject to something positive, a topic that everyone loved. At lunch, Frank picked up a drink for Mark, sat it on the desk, and said, "Sorry, man." It wasn't Frank's fault, but apologies aren't about who's right and who's wrong. Apologies are simply a way to plug the leak.

Emotion has unbelievable power. Mark's emotion stirred the whole shop. But so did Frank's. Frank exercised his power and changed the course not just for himself, but for everyone. He refused to ride the roller coaster of emotion yet again. How many times had the shop ridden this roller coaster? How many times had Mark's emotion leaked all over the others? How many mechanics had quit their jobs? But it stopped with Frank. Instead of holding on for the ride, Frank unbuckled his belt and stepped aside. He decided to plug the leak. He stopped his own emotions before the leak turned into a flood. He plugged the leak for the others in the room. Then he went to the source and tried to plug that leak as well. His actions stopped the leak from turning into a flood and destroying all in its path. Frank's actions had long lasting impacts. Dan never quit his job, probably because Frank plugged his leak. Dan still works in the shop, quite happily. Mark still slams doors and occasionally throws tools, but for the most part, the others no longer ride the roller coaster, because Frank has become an expert at plugging leaks, a truly worthwhile skill.

Sometimes, as with Frank, a simple fix will work. You might just need a small act of kindness or a word of understanding. This is always worth a try because if you catch a leak quick enough, it can keep the flood from coming. You can't always fix a leak immediately. Sometimes you have to attempt the repair over and over using multiple methods. Sometimes you just need to dry off, give it time, and treat the person who is leaking as you normally would until he gets over it himself.

We need to learn how to plug leaks (see the "Life Jackets" chapter for more strategies). We also need to learn to expect emotion. Expect people to get mad when they're faced with life's frustrations or when they don't get something they want. Expect people to get mad when they feel we have done something wrong, whether we have or not. Expect people to be upset, even when it doesn't make sense to us. Don't let emotion become contagious, unless it's positive emotion. When your spouse is mad, don't get mad in return. When your boss is upset, don't get upset too. When your teenager slams her door, don't barge through it in your fury. Plug the leaks. First plug yours, then try to plug theirs. It's a wonderful skill that can change your life!

HOW TO APPLY THIS TO YOUR LIFE:

Whose emotion do you allow to leak onto you? Some of us allow *all* emotion from anyone to leak onto us. When someone gets mad, we get mad back. When someone says we hurt them, we feel hurt too. If this is you, admit to yourself that you allow almost everyone to leak onto you. For others, there are a few people to whom we react the most. Often it is a spouse, child, parent, or boss. Who leaks on you?

Think of the last time you reacted to being leaked on. **What could you have done to plug the leak for yourself in that situation?** Write down at least 5 ways you think you could help plug your own leaks and keep emotion from growing inside you.

Think of a time when someone's emotion leaked on those around you. Maybe it is the same situation you just thought of. **What could you have said or done to plug the leak for others?** You might want to use some of Frank's tactics (changing the subject, saying "Sorry, man," etc). Write down at least 5 things you could use to help plug the leaks and keep the negative flood of emotion from destroying people.

5

PMS
Preference, Mistake, or Sin?

"Much that we call evil is really good in disguises; and we should not quarrel rashly with adversities not yet understood, nor overlook the mercies often bound up in them." Horace Mann

We women (hang in there, men) know that there are biological forces at work against us. Even after years of marriage, I'm amazed how, at certain times of the month, I might actually say something like, "You don't even love me!" My husband will then put his arm around me and sweetly reply, "Don't worry, honey. I'll love you in about three days." While this would be highly offensive to most women, I actually find it helpful because I realize, "Wow, I'm absolutely crazy right now and in three days these hormones will be gone." Indeed, we are crazy in many situations in life, and I'm convinced it's because we *all* have PMS. Now, when we think of PMS, we might imagine someone who is emotional and overly sensitive or someone who is angry and on the war path. These ideas are true, even though I'm talking now about a very different kind of PMS. I'm talking about *Preferences, Mistakes,* and *Sin.*

There are times in life when people actually do things that are wrong. I try to allow God to decide what is right and wrong, so I go by the Ten Commandments: it's wrong to steal and wrong to murder. There are some things in life that are just wrong, and these fall into the category of *sin.* When someone sins against me, I can get pretty crazy.

There are also *mistakes.* Have you ever written a bad check? Ever made a driving error? It's not a *sin.* There is no moral issue here; it's just an honest mistake. My mistakes might look different from yours, but we all make them. Sometimes I still go a little crazy when people make mistakes.

Then there is a third category—a huge, gigantic, enormous, all-encompassing category called *preferences.* Most of the time our arguments aren't about *mistakes* or *sin*: they're really about *preferences.*

Albert Ellis, a famous therapist, often said that **we've got to quit *should-ing* all over everybody.** We do this, don't we? "He *shouldn't* have done that!" "She *should* be more careful!" "You *shouldn't* pile your dishes in the sink,

> *...we've got to quit should-ing all over everybody.*

that's so inconsiderate!" But really, there isn't a "should." Really, there's only a preference: "I would *prefer* that you put your dishes in the dishwasher instead of the sink." There is no commandment that says, "Thou shalt put thy dishes in the dishwasher instead of piling them in the sink." The fact of the matter is that I *prefer* the dishes go in the dishwasher, but my son *prefers* to put them in the sink.

I once asked my son, "Are you aware that we own a dishwasher?" He seems to be fully capable of getting the dishes to the sink but cannot manage the extra ten seconds it would take to actually put them into the dishwasher. I cannot understand because "I would never do that." I would never put dishes in the sink. I would put them directly into the dishwasher. That's how I operate. That is my *preference*.

But he doesn't care if the dishes are in the dishwasher or not. He doesn't *value* it like I do; it's just not important to him. So now we have a problem on our hands, because I believe I should be able to walk up to you, rub my magic lamp, and you—my little genie—will pop out and grant my wishes! I say, "Sweetie, please put your dishes in the dishwasher," and you grant me my wish! Or I say, "Honey, don't put your keys on the dining room table," and you grant me my wish! The problem is that I've been rubbing this lamp for a long, *long* time now, and nobody pops out and asks me for my wishes.

So what do we do when people don't do what we want? Usually we get mad at them and we "talk" to them about it and usually not in a very productive way. What might be smarter is to realize when anger is actually merited and when it is not. When sins are committed or mistakes are repeated, we need to solve a problem and anger might very well be merited, but most "problems" don't actually need solving. Why? Because **most "problems" are just** *preferences.*

> *...most "problems" are just* preferences.

A friend of mine had talked with her husband about her plans for them to paint the living room on Saturday. But when Saturday came and she had just finished taping off all the windows and doors, her husband emerged with guitar case in hand and announced that he was going to band practice. So he left, and she was fuming mad. She finished painting what she could in the living room and went outside for a ladder to do the rest, but she couldn't get the ladder down because it was too high for her to reach, so she couldn't finish painting. Disappointed, she slumped right down on the ground outside.

Her neighbor, Tom, was over in his yard pulling weeds. Being the fatherly neighbor that Tom is, he came over to check on her. "You okay?" he said.

She brightened up a little bit and said, "Well, Tom, I could sure use some help getting this ladder down!" As he was getting the ladder, she saw an opportunity. She knew that Tom worked in construction and did professional painting. She began making small talk and asked about the gardening: "The garden looks great, Tom. Maybe I can give you a hand with those weeds. But I just have to finish painting my living room …Hey, if you want to, you could help me finish it up, then we could tackle those weeds together!"

Tom politely declined the offer and went on his way, while she went back into the house, still fuming mad at her husband. Suddenly, a thought dawned on her: "When Tom told me he couldn't paint today, I didn't care at all, but when my husband did the same, it was a huge deal." So many times the people we love the most don't get to have a life because we rub our lamp and say, "Hey, honey, on Saturday we're painting the living room!"—and in our minds, it's a done deal. My friend realized the high expectations she was placing on her spouse and on her children, and she made up something that she called "The Neighbor Rule." **The Neighbor Rule says: "If I wouldn't be mad at my neighbor for it, then I won't be mad at my spouse."** How is it that we can give our next-door neighbor, and even complete strangers, more respect, freedom, and courtesy than we give to the ones we love the most?

I force myself to say "I prefer" all the time as a reminder, because it's way too easy to say, "He *should* have called! How selfish!" or "He *should* be helping me paint the living room right now. He's my husband, he's *supposed* to help me!" It's not your husband's job in life to be your magic genie. Be your own magic genie—if you want it, you're responsible for it. It's true that sometimes what you want will involve someone else; perhaps you want time

…respect others by making requests, not demands.

together with your spouse or you want all your kids to be at home for a family night. In these cases, we can still **respect others by making requests, not demands**.

A request means the answer is allowed to be "no." Authors Cloud and Townsend of the popular *Boundaries* books say, "You must be free to say no before you can wholeheartedly say yes.[2]" Are the people in your life really free to say "no" to you without fear of you being upset by it? Or do they feel like they have to comply with your request to avoid your negative consequences? Whether you think someone "should" or "should not" do something, your only option is to ask, never demand, and give the other person the freedom to decline your request.[3] Sometimes asking gets a "no," and we may simply need to make other arrangements. Sometimes we don't get what we want because we don't arrange things to be able to have it. But ultimately, at the end of the day, we give our neighbor the respect, courtesy, and freedom to say "no" to us. Why can't we do the same with our spouse, kids, and coworkers? Why must we turn everything into a moral issue? The truth is that if you *prefer* to spend your Saturday painting and your husband *prefers* to spend his Saturday at band practice, this is *not* a right or wrong issue. This is a *preference* issue, as most things are, and the good news is that you have power over those preferences, power to keep them from turning into ugly, nasty, misery-making *shoulds*.

This applies when others are working on tasks as well. We can allow them the freedom to do it how they see fit, which might be differently than how we would have done it. We may have used a pie chart instead of a bar chart for that presentation. Maybe adding a little more of this spice or that might be worth trying? Perhaps clothes still get clean even if the jeans are with the towels. Even how someone drives is simply a preference; it is not "wrong." While we might think so at times, there isn't a morally "right" way to do most things. There might be instructions given by a manufacturer, but even that is just one way to do something, a way you might "prefer," but still just one way. **It's amazing how many things in life are really just *preferences*.**

HOW TO APPLY THIS TO YOUR LIFE:

Now that you've figured out what PMS really stands for—Preferences, Mistakes, and Sin—it's time to figure out what you've been getting angry, frustrated, and upset about that isn't really wrong at all. Perhaps it's the way your kid's coach runs basketball drills, or how your spouse leaves laundry on the floor, or how your co-worker talks so loudly you can't think. **What have you been getting angry, frustrated, or upset about that is truly just a preference?**

You *should* not leave your dishes in the sink. You *should* not park in the handicapped parking space. You *should* speak up during meetings. You *should* spend your day with the family. **What's your list of SHOULDS that causes you to "should all over people?"** Be honest; if you are anything like me, I bet there are quite a few!

There are some people we give a free pass to, aren't there? We get angry at our loved ones, but let the neighbor across the street that we barely know off the hook. Interesting, isn't it? Who are the people in your life who do <u>not</u> get those free passes? **How will you get yourself to extend "The Neighbor Rule" to your spouse, coworker, child, mother-in-law . . . and let them off the hook?**

Now the big question is: **what are you going to do to stop *should*-ing on people?** Is it extending "The Neighbor Rule"? Is it saying "I prefer" instead of "you should"? Is it pinching yourself every time the word "should" comes out of your mouth to remind yourself that you've said it once again?

6

Q-Tip
Translating well

"We tend to judge others by their behavior, and ourselves by our intentions."
Albert F. Schlieder

When I grade student papers and make corrections, my thought is not, "Wow, you're unbelievably dumb!" Rather, I'm usually thinking about how great they're doing, but that they just need a little fix here or there. The comments I put on their papers do not indicate that I'm thinking poorly of my students; they're just instances of me thinking out loud, such as "I'm not following you here" or "Add citation." My role is to help them improve and learn, and part of learning is understanding what is incorrect, so that you can correct it in the future. Yet, at times, these comments are translated by students as insults instead of suggestions. **Translation is the key. We need to learn to translate with good intentions and assume the best of people.**

> Translation is the key. We need to learn to translate with good intentions and assume the best of people.

Many conversations viewed as critical by the receiver are *not* viewed as critical by the giver: the meaning is lost in translation. The giver typically views the exchange as a helpful suggestion, a request, or useful information. The receiver would benefit greatly from changing their thoughts from "They are criticizing me" or "They are insulting me" to "They are making suggestions or giving information." This nuance, this slight change of language, has the potential to eliminate a great deal of misery. Just think if my students would choose to translate my notes as "My professor is trying to help me to be my best" rather than "My professor thinks I'm an idiot." The negative view leaves students feeling wounded and wronged, while the alternative view leaves them feeling valued and loved.

We've all done this. We all translate certain moments as negative when the speaker did not intend the words negatively at all. We experience these moments every day. How we translate these moments is the key! I wonder how often we mistakenly translate "Let me help you" moments as "I can't believe you are so stupid, let me correct you" moments.

I know I fail in translating often. I once emailed my sister-in-law, and after a few days with no response, I immediately began wondering what I'd done to offend her or why she didn't like me, instead of thinking how busy she must be with *five boys*. Our default mode is to assume that the other person intended to slight us. But, of course, when *we* offer suggestions, we view ourselves as helpful. We know our own intentions, so we realize we are not being unkind. But we don't have access to others' inner thoughts as we do our own, and so we fear the worst.

Worse still, we tend to be even more sensitive when we lack the energy to process the situation. Thus, the more stress we are under, the more likely we are to negatively translate a situation as a slight against us, rather than as an understandable situation. But in most cases, there really are understandable circumstances, and people are not intentionally trying to be cold or difficult.

As Maureen Killoran of SpiritQuest Coaching wrote, "Quit Taking It Personally! The kids who don't call often enough probably really *are* busy (and didn't you raise them to be independent?) Q-Tip It! Got a spouse, friend, kid, or coworker who seems to ignore the things you say? Odds are, they probably *are* hard of hearing, forgetful, busy, or caught up in their own priorities, rather than intentionally trying to drive you crazy. Q-Tip It! Quit Taking It Personally! **Choose to be the solution, instead of the finger pointer.[4]**" Most of what's going on in a person's life *is* situational and has nothing to do with you.

There is a lady in my church who's been married for forty years, and her husband-well, I don't know any non-colorful words to describe him-so let's just call him a tough, old guy. I've known him my whole life, and often he would walk into the house, smack his wife on the rear, and call her fat, ugly, or stupid. Needless to say, this created just a little bit of winter in her heart after a while. Their relationship grew cold, gray, and distant.

One day, this tough, old guy's dear friend came over to the house to return an air compressor he had borrowed. The wife was very eager to meet him because her husband talked about his friend night and day. She knew that her husband loved this guy and thought he walked on water. But just after his friend dropped off the compressor and was getting into his truck to leave, she noticed something rather interesting. Her husband said, "Hey you *blankety-blank*, get your *blankety-blank* off my property!" To which the guy replied, "Right back at ya!" with a smile on his face! And it finally dawned on her. Her husband has a very unique way of expressing love, now doesn't he?

And so, as usual, he came in the house, smacked her on the rear, and called her a fat *blankety-blank*, but this time, she chose to say, "Love you too." He looked at her and smiled and gave her a kiss on the cheek. This became their new routine, and what had been a long, cold winter turned into summer again.

On their thirtieth wedding anniversary, her husband planned a surprise for her. Without her knowing, he scheduled for them to renew their vows. Keep in mind that he is an ornery old cuss, and if I had not actually seen it with my own two eyes, I would never, *ever* believe that this guy had actually scheduled to renew his vows. But summertime came again. All those years he was saying "I love you" in the only way he knew how. Once she took notice and chose to give love back, the decades-long arctic blizzard melted away, and beautiful summertime came again!

But what if someone actually *is* being intentionally hurtful?

"He hurt my feelings." "She made me so mad!" "They drive me crazy!" We say things like this all the time, don't we? But it's really our choice how we translate. People don't make us mad. People don't hurt our feelings. It's our translations of what they say that create the hurt. For example, let's imagine some guy says, "Mike, you're a big, ugly jerk." Mike replies, "Whatever." This same guy then turns to Joe and says, "Joe, you're a big, ugly jerk." Joe becomes very hurt and upset: "Can you believe that guy called me a big, ugly jerk?!" The words were not the issue for poor Joe; while we might think these unkind words cause anger, the words themselves didn't cause the anger. Mike heard those same words and didn't think a thing of it. Joe's anger comes from within himself, from how he translates those incoming words. Mike's translation was simply "whatever," But Joe's translation resulted in him feeling insulted.

The way we translate a situation leads to our anger—not what the other person says or does. No one *makes* you mad. No one *makes* you sad. As Eleanor Roosevelt is attributed with saying, "No one can make you feel inferior without your consent.[5]" And since we have the power over how we choose to translate, we can ultimately choose joy, peace, patience, and kindness even in the face of ugliness. Even when someone is lashing out in their anger, we can translate their actions as "He's upset and saying things he doesn't mean" instead of "How dare he say that!?" Whether it's because they are upset in the moment, trying to get back at you, or provoking you to get attention, we can translate in ways that lead us to respond with patience instead of returning the ugliness. In the end, who among us doesn't want patience and kindness? How many times have we been fired upon and, translating that action as war, we fought back, choosing to say or do things we later regretted?

I remember a time when my daughter and I were talking in the kitchen, and I noticed a cake baking in the oven. To me, it appeared to be done, and if left much longer, might end up overdone. So I reminded my daughter to take the cake out of the oven. My daughter's translation in that moment was, "My mom thinks I'm an idiot." My actual thought in that moment was, "I forget things like this all the time, and I know she doesn't want to burn the cake." I was not viewing her negatively; I was actually thinking of myself and how forgetful I can be about taking things out of the oven. Unfortunately, that's not how she took it at the time. But now, years later, if I remind her of something, her response is very different and usually includes a "Thanks." My daughter has learned how to translate well.

I bet you've already done this too. I bet there are things in your life now that ten years ago would have really set you off. But because you've matured, those things don't push your buttons the same way that they used to. You see, the *event* isn't what caused all that emotion ten years ago. *You* caused that emotion for yourself by how you chose to translate that event! Maybe you can even think of a relationship you had ten years ago with someone you just couldn't stand, who really got on your nerves. Over the years they've remained the same—just as rude and insensitive as they used to be—but it doesn't bother you as much anymore. You have learned to command your own emotions. You *can* translate, and you probably already have!

HOW TO APPLY THIS TO YOUR LIFE:

Criticism is 100% perspective. Think back to a situation in the past few weeks when you felt like someone was criticizing you. Perhaps you were offended by this person's words. What was your perspective at the time?

Now choose to look at it from a different perspective. How can you change the translation of what was said to you to have a better understanding of what was intended or what was really going on? **How might you change your translation?**

Is there something that your spouse, child, or coworker does that drives you nuts? In fact, you just know they're doing it on purpose in order to drive you crazy—or are they? What do you need to Q-Tip? **I need to "Quit Taking It Personally" when….**

Instead of taking it personally, I will…

You have a choice. Have you ever caught yourself saying, "He just makes me so angry" or "I can't help it that she makes me so mad." If you've ever done this, do you realize that you are giving the other person an awful lot of credit for "making" you feel a certain way? I say give credit where credit's due! You are the one choosing to be angry. But no worries! You can choose to ignore it, respond positively, take a time-out, dance a jig—whatever you want—in place of that anger. Think about the last time you responded in anger to something someone said or did. How could you have responded instead of in anger?

How would that have benefited you?

7

Seasons
Going forward even in the dead of winter

"However long the night, the dawn will break." Unknown

We all go through seasons in our relationships. When we're dating, it's summertime; we're having a blast, and everything is warm and wonderful. Once autumn comes, things start to "fall" apart on us. And then it's the dead of winter. What do we do when it's cold and gray and desolate? We hibernate and seclude ourselves. And when we're disturbed like a sleeping bear from our cold hibernation, watch out! A lot of winters walk into my counseling office.

We need to expect winters. Sometimes winter comes because our relationship has deteriorated, and we've allowed autumn to turn into winter. Sometimes winter comes because life's circumstances have depleted, destroyed, and emptied us. For a long time, every single couple that came to see me, whether they were twenty or fifty, had kids under the age of five. Why? Because children are amazing, fabulous, precious, little life-draining creations. Many things—a child, a new boss, a job, a sick parent, or a never-ending project—can drain the life out of us and lead our relationships into a deep winter. Our relationships almost always end up in winter at some point, often more than once.

But I have wonderful news: a little sunshine can melt a lot of snow pretty quickly. Even when there's been a blizzard and all we can see is snow and ice, it's amazing the layers we can melt away with our warmth. I (Shannon) knew a family that had experienced a tragedy, and as a result, the teenage daughter had been behaving poorly. She was taking drugs, drinking, partying, failing school, and getting into vehement arguments with her parents, all at the ripe old age of thirteen. So, in the midst of dealing with the pain of their tragedy, the family experienced even more pain as they watched their daughter self-destruct.

The effects were far-reaching. The parents were not seeing eye-to-eye, siblings were coming to blows, and the relationship between the teenage daughter and the parents was quickly disintegrating. The father was an "It's my way or the highway" kind of man. However, that particular approach was not working very well with his daughter. The more he laid down the law, the more she fought back. It was the dead of winter in their home. Every relationship in their family was suffering.

The father and I talked about a new way to approach his daughter, but this wasn't a change that was going to happen overnight. Dad thought that raising his daughter the way he was raised, with an iron fist, was the best way. But after we looked at how well that was working—and it was *not* working well—he was open to making some slight changes. He chose to really *see* his daughter: her passions, how she communicated, what she was doing well, what made her happy, what made her sad…and then he chose to respond accordingly. You see, one of the main problems was that the daughter didn't think her father loved her, which she announced in a family meeting. Ouch! He was hurt, confused, and at a total loss for solutions. But Dad didn't want the winter any longer; he wanted spring in this relationship. He was tired of the fighting and the constant punishments, which weren't even working. Do you know what he did? He started speaking words of affirmation, his daughter's love language, as outlined in the book *The 5 Love Languages* by Dr. Gary Chapman. And boy, did he get good at speaking her love language! He started telling her what she was doing well instead of only concentrating on what she was always doing wrong. The impact was amazing! He then started allowing her to earn privileges that she'd once thought would be out of reach. They went from a blizzard to sunshine! But it took time and effort and a complete change in his approach. **Even if we don't see results quickly, when we consciously choose to be different, when we choose warmth, eventually winter *will* melt into summer again.**

> *Even if we don't see results quickly, when we consciously choose to be different, when we choose warmth, eventually winter will melt into summer again.*

And don't forget to celebrate those small signs of spring along the way—the daffodil that pokes its head out of the snow, signaling that more sunshine is coming. Air Force Chaplain John Painter learned an important lesson about celebration from his four-year-old nephew, William, on a family bowling excursion:

> "The adults were very competitive. If we knocked down eight pins, we would feel obliged to explain what went wrong—why we didn't knock down all ten. We focused on technique and tried to tweak

our form. The older children in the next lane had apparently learned some of this from us, as they would walk away disappointed when they knocked down only a few pins. But four-year-old William would jump for joy and offer high fives and hugs all around on every occasion that he knocked down any pins at all, even if it was only one! William knew the value and importance of celebrating the smallest accomplishment, a lesson the adults needed to learn again. He taught us the importance of celebrating what we did do, and not wallowing in angst over that small slice of unmet accomplishment."

As I share these success stories, I am aware that some of you are living in an arctic winter right now. Please don't think that I am diminishing the pain that comes in winter, because there are some truly terrible things in life that drive us there. Sometimes we have been wronged and deeply hurt. Sometimes what was done to us was awful. But I have found that even those in the deepest pain never regret the choice to melt the snow and ice, even though they may not have felt like it at first; even when every ounce of them didn't want to, they still chose to be warm.

If you choose to be the ray of sun in your relationship, even if you have been deeply and undeservedly hurt, not only will it melt their heart, it will melt your own. *Positive feelings follow positive action.* This is hard to believe at first, but if you try it, you will see. Choose to do what is wise and loving, regardless of how you feel, and wise and loving feelings will follow. **Love, and you will get more love. However, the reverse is also true: unkindness and distance will get you more of the same.** You've heard it before: love is what you do, not how you feel. **Love acts kind, even when it doesn't feel kind.** Love demonstrates trust and grace, even when it doesn't feel trusting or graceful. We have to give it to get it. This is easier said than done. At times it seems near impossible, and you will win some and lose some as you commit to this course of action.

Love, and you will get more love. However, the reverse is also true: unkindness and distance will get you more of the same.

Keep in mind that when there are layers upon layers of ice and snow, winter may continue for a while. Have the courage to keep shining your ray of warmth. It takes a lot of sun to melt away those layers, but keep on shining because spring and summer are worth it! No one consciously chooses winter over summer in a relationship, yet sometimes our actions are the very things that keep us there. Sometimes we are waiting for the other person to show kindness or ask for forgiveness, and by waiting, we remain in the blizzard. The other person may not have the knowledge or the skills to shine again, but *you do*. You can choose to melt away the snow, and in doing so, you will one day bask in the warmth of the summer sun.

HOW TO APPLY THIS TO YOUR LIFE:

Sometimes you just don't feel like being nice, right? We all have days when the thought of being nice to every person who crosses our path makes us cringe. But you just learned that right feeling follows right action. It's worth a try if it will actually make you feel better. **What are some small ways you can commit to shining your sun and being warm even when you don't feel like it or even when it isn't deserved?**

Now for the difficult one. **What can you do to keep shining warmth through the winter even when it seems like the snow will never melt?** Maybe you keep silent while your boss rants and raves, or maybe you make welcoming small talk with someone who hasn't spoken to you in days. Perhaps you leave little notes of kindness, cook a favorite meal, bring coffee to her cubicle, or help him out with something you know will make an impact (wash a car, finish that report, do their chores). Just be ready to persevere, and don't expect a warm return for a while.

Look closely for the smallest bud of spring in your relationship. **What positive things can you choose to celebrate today?**

8

Life Jackets
Moving beyond the issue to settle the emotion

"Most people do not listen with the intent to understand; they listen with the intent to reply." Stephen R. Covey

One summer I was taking care of an absolutely fearless little boy named Johnny. The house I grew up in had a pool in the backyard, and when Johnny arrived, he ran and jumped right into the deep end. I saw him bobbing up and down, going under the water, coming back up and saying "Nealy!" and then going down again and bobbing back up. "Nealy…I can't--!" After a few bobs, I realized Johnny was telling me that he couldn't swim! So I scooped him up out of the water and pointed him toward the shallow end.

While Johnny was drowning, would it have done him any good if I had stood at the edge of the pool giving him instructions on how to swim? I could have told him the "right" way to do it or explained to him how he was "wrong" and "shouldn't" flail his hands. I technically would have been correct in saying, "Move your arms like this! No, not like that, like this!"—but how absurd would that be?

And yet we do these things all the time in our relationships. People are drowning in their emotion but we insist on giving them instructions, telling them the "right" way and explaining how they are "wrong" and "shouldn't" do something. But this is not the time to teach or criticize them or to solve problems. **When they are drowning in emotion and the conflict is escalating, help them out. They don't need a lecture—they need a life jacket!**

When they are drowning in emotion and the conflict is escalating, help them out.

Our conflicts usually start out about the problem, but when emotion enters the picture, the conflict soon becomes about the emotion. We are no longer talking about the real issue; instead we are defending ourselves ("I didn't mean it like that"), deflecting attention away from ourselves ("But *you* did *this*"), or minimizing the situation ("It's really no big deal"). When this happens, we have to stop talking about the issue and start managing the emotion. We cannot solve the problem until the emotions are under control. It is useless to rationalize with a drowning person. You have to make them feel safe again. Once Johnny felt safe, I could teach him how to swim. Once the other person feels safe and is no longer drowning in emotion, you can focus on solving the problem.

Everyone's drowning looks different, so you must learn to detect signs of drowning in the other person. People tend to go one of two ways, silence or violence, and we have to look for those cues in order to be effective. Some people are very matter-of-fact; because they don't rant and rave, their drowning is more difficult to see. The fight may not be very loud, and their words may be very logical and factual, but the other party is still feeling threatened. You may find someone in your life has certain phrases they use when they are upset, such as: "It doesn't matter anyway," "Never mind," "I knew I shouldn't have told you," or "You don't understand!" These are the same people who might start flailing their hands, get red faced, or increase their volume. Our more quiet types may try to change the subject or use nonverbal cues such as crossing their arms, going silent, or walking away.

How can we make them feel safe again so that we can get this problem solved?

- **Apologize**: "I'm sorry that we've gotten to this point. I must not have said that very well."
- **Listen**: "It sounds like you feel I'm just trying to get my way, but I really want to know what's important to you too. What are you thinking right now?" Then actually be quiet and listen.
- **Empathize**: Empathy focuses entirely on what the other person is feeling, not on what we think or feel. "You seem angry..." or "That seems hurtful to you..." are great empathic statements which can help drain that emotion away.
- **Ask questions**: They can help you draw out more of their heart: "So when you found out that I didn't do x, what did you want to do?"
- **Reflect understanding**: "So let's see if I'm hearing you right: you think I'm being too eager and that we should think it through some more? Is that right?"
- **Validate**: "Well, I can see your point. If I thought that someone was trying to take advantage of me, I would feel angry about that too."
- **Encourage**: "You know, you're such a smart kid, and you have so much going for you, I just know you're going to do great things in life. I know you'll figure out how to get your homework in because

you're a smart kid, and you know failing classes will hurt you in the long run." (By the way, this is what I call a "sandwich"—you've got the meat in the middle and the nice soft bread on both sides. Keep in mind that this soft, fluffy bread is not dishonest fluff, but encouraging words reminding them of their value in your eyes.)

- **Offer options or solutions that the other person would like**: "Would it help to do *x* or *y*?" If not, then "What do you think might help?"
- **Give them time and space**: Sometimes people need to step back and think. Solving the issue in the moment is overwhelming for them, and the most effective way to deal with their emotion is to step away and process it themselves.

Bottom line: we must learn how to stop the chaos of emotion and help the other person feel safe again, because if we can stop it, we can solve it. We cannot move forward as long as we are full of emotion. Think of a swimming pool again—have you ever tried to run in water that's up to your neck? If we are trying to move forward in deep water, we're not going to get very far or get there very fast. But if we can drain the water down until we're standing in about one foot, then we can really get moving. Similarly, we have to drain off the emotion before we can create solutions.

Also, keep in mind that while *you* may be standing in a foot of water, the other person may be drowning in emotion ten feet deep! Maybe you think they shouldn't feel that way—that they shouldn't be drowning—but this isn't about determining who's right and who's wrong. The simple fact is that we cannot expect that person to move forward with us when they are up to their neck in emotion. We must make it safe for them so that they can drain this emotion away. For example, if every time I walk into a room, you hit me in the head with a hammer, I'm going to stop walking into that room. If every time we talk about finances, you tell me I'm wrong, I will likely avoid the topic (silence) or approach it defensively (violence). But if, when I share my opinions this time, you listen and understand and empathize and validate, then you've just pulled the plug on all my emotions! The more effectively you can pull the plug on emotion, the quicker you will be able to move forward toward a win-win solution.

Let's say the boss expects Tom to meet him today at 1:00 p.m., and he's late. Tom is always late. The boss is sitting there, stewing in his emotion, when Tom walks in the door. "I thought you were going to be here at 1:00!" he shouts. Let's say that, instead of defending himself or explaining there was a wreck on the interstate holding up traffic, Tom recognizes his boss is up to his neck in emotion and that he needs to drain it off before they can have a conversation.

Tom:　"I'm sorry I'm late. I know this is an important meeting." (Apologizing and Validating)

Boss:　"Darn right, it's important! You know what's on the line here! How could you!?" (You pulled a plug there, and a little emotion drained away. We don't expect him to respond with immediate calm. It takes a little more than that.)

Tom:　"I can understand why you're upset. I know I tend to be late." (Validating)

Boss:　"Tend to be? I wish you weren't late all the time! You're never here on time!" (You maybe got a little water out there.)

Tom:　"You've worked countless hours to make this happen. I can imagine how upset you must be. What can I do first? Do you want the earnings report or the profit margin slides?" (Encouragement and Offering Options) (You hit the gusher on that one. All the emotion drains away. You can see the anger disappear and hear a sigh of relief.)

Boss:　"Let's start with the earnings."

Tom never defended himself, and he never disagreed with his boss. He also never talked about the fact that he had run into traffic, though there may be a time to do this later. Sometimes information can also help defuse the emotion. But here, he doesn't even mention it. It doesn't matter. The boss is up to his ears in emotion and wouldn't have heard it anyway. It would have seemed like another one of Tom's excuses. Maybe later Tom could share that he actually left thirty minutes earlier than he thought was necessary in order to arrive before the meeting began. This would probably be more helpful later, when the boss could hear it and sense Tom's effort to improve. Only after we first deal with the emotion can we deal with the situation and move forward with our game plan.

HOW TO APPLY THIS TO YOUR LIFE:

Think of times when the people in your life have been drowning in emotion. What does that look like for each of them?

Which of the tools (life jackets) above could you put in your own personal toolbox to help you have more productive conversations?

How could you start using these tools immediately?

Think of a recent argument in which you were emotionally exchanging defenses and accusations—spinning your tires and getting nowhere fast. If you had been trying to drain the other person's emotion, what would you have said differently? Choose your tools and list three approaches.

Further reading:
> Patterson, Kerry, et al. *Crucial Conversations: Tools for Talking When Stakes Are High.* New York: McGraw-Hill, 2002.
> Patterson, Kerry, Joseph Grenny, Ron McMillan, and Al Switzler. *Crucial Confrontations.* First edition. Columbus: McGraw-Hill, 2004.

9

Welcome to the Jungle
How to relate to different personalities

> *"A pessimist sees the difficulty in every opportunity; an optimist sees the opportunity in every difficulty." Winston Churchill*

Have you ever felt like you married the wrong person? Or that you couldn't possibly like or even get along with a coworker or family member? In these situations, most of us tend to view the other person as the problem. I don't know how many times I've looked on at another person's behavior with horror, anger, or sheer disbelief. Common phrases that come to mind are: "What were they thinking?" "I just don't get it!" and "How could they do that?!" Actor David Duchovny once said, "The key is to trust people to be who they are. Instead, we trust people to be who we want them to be, and when they aren't, we cry.[6]"

I (Shannon) have taught group fitness classes for years. During class, Ana does not like for the fans to run on her side of the studio when she's working out. She wants a good sweat. Diane knows this, but she thinks that all fans should be on all of the time. Every week, Diane complains and is upset that Ana does not want those fans on, even though she already knows Ana's going to keep them turned off!

We all do this, don't we? There are moments when we expect a person to say or do something differently—how we would say or do it—and are disappointed when they do not. But in reality, we should "expect Ana to be Ana." And Ana likes the fans off. Furthermore, we can accept Ana as a valuable person with all her differences, even though we would prefer that Ana keep the fans on.

One day I came across a book that would forever change my life, allowing me to trust people to be exactly who they are. *The Two Sides of Love* by Drs. Gary Smalley and John Trent discusses four types of people and names them after animals, which are outlined in these chapters.[7] I like the animal association because each of us already has a basic understanding of these animals: the Lion, the Otter, the Golden Retriever, and the Beaver. Therefore, we can get an idea of what each personality may be like. Each person we know has unique tendencies, both strengths and weaknesses; even the people who drive us completely crazy have aspects of their personality that are truly remarkable if we only know what to look for and where to look.

We all have a little of each animal in us, and we can all act like any animal at any given time. However, we tend to have a primary and a secondary personality type. These are the ways we relate to the world in most circumstances. Some people even have competing types; one type may be people focused and the other task focused. At times, these types wrestle within. And then there are a few people who are mainly one personality type. Knowing which personality type you are and that of others can benefit you in every relationship. So which personality are you? You can take this short personality test to see which animal you are: http://smalley.cc/free-personality-test. This is just a quick test but will typically assess us correctly *if we answer honestly.* However, as you read on, you may get a good picture of which animal you, and those you encounter, tend to be most often.

LIONS

Lions are the kings of the jungle, or at least they like to be. They tend to take charge and tell other people what to do, and sometimes how to do it. They see what they want and go after it. They are very decisive, persistent creatures. They tend to catch anything they chase because they persevere, no matter what obstacles arise. While this persistence is a great strength, it can also be a great weakness, as Lions can be stubborn, dominating, and unwilling to yield when they have their minds set on something. It's "my way or the highway" for the Lion, and if you get in their way, they might just roar and sink their teeth into you. They will also roar if you don't get things done and done quickly; remember that they are task focused and fast paced. When a Lion is stressed or in conflict, they have a tendency to be overly controlling, think "drill sergeant."

Lions have a superman mentality. They are efficient and effective at work, able to leap tall buildings in a single bound. They think they can do anything, and, because of their persistence, they usually can. Lions are made of steel and often forget that others are not so steely, hence the insensitivity. When a woman approached a group of friends, little did she know a Lion was in their midst. She was proud of her new, very colorful dress and asked, "So, ladies, what do you think?" and twirled around to indicate her dress. The Lion, verbal and quick, was the first to speak: "Looks like my 3-year-old went crazy on you with his crayons." The Lion did not intend to hurt the woman when she spoke these words. After all, the Lion wouldn't have been hurt if someone had said this to her. Lions speak in facts, not feelings. On the one hand, Lions are very honest and up front. On the other hand, Lions are very honest and up front!

What Lions care about is what's going on right now and what action needs to be done to get the results they want. They aren't into details or long stories. They will want the reader's digest version with the punch line first.

TIPS FOR DEALING WITH A LION:

- *Expect a Lion to act exactly like a Lion*. The more you expect a Lion to act like a kitty cat, the more frustrated you will be with them. They are quick to speak and act, focused only on accomplishing the task, not on relating to people. Try not to take it personally.
- *Speak the language of a Lion.* The language of a Lion is forward and direct. Give them the facts, and get right to the point.
- *Lions are motivated by challenge and results*. If you want to persuade and motivate a Lion, show them (quickly) how what you are wanting is connected to the results they want.

ADVICE FOR A LION:

Lions tend to ignore the requests, suggestions, opinions, and feelings of others. If you want real results, you must eventually learn the skills of *listening* and *validating* when others speak. Listen when your coworker brings a fresh idea to the table; even if it's *your* team that you created and spearheaded, you did pick her for a reason. Hear what she has to say. She may bring up a valuable concept that gets the results you want. Validate your teenager when she is concerned about a situation with friends at school. Let her know you *do* realize it's a big deal to her. Your results will increase exponentially when you learn to relate better.

OTTERS

Have you ever seen an otter at the zoo? If you see them from far off, they're usually lounging in the sun, kicking back, relaxing. But when you walk closer and stand in front of the glass, what do they do? They start swimming and flipping in the water, playing and chasing each other. They love to entertain, and they'll do anything for an audience. Otters speak the language of fun; they are the true party animals of the animal kingdom. They're personable, optimistic, enthusiastic, and full of energy.

They will inspire and influence you, which can sometimes mean that they will talk you into things you didn't want to do with all the charisma of a cult leader. They're usually good with words and quick to make promises, though sometimes lack the follow-through to keep those promises. When Otters are under stress or in conflict, they are likely to lash out and personally attack you. Because they are incredible influencers, they know how to push your buttons and will get you to change your mind if they can.

Unlike the Lion, they are people focused rather than task focused. They enjoy plenty of involvement with others. They don't care much about getting things done, unless it's fun and you'll do it with them. However, like the Lion, they're quick to decide and quick to speak, so they tend to be rather impulsive. These are the people who go out to pick up drive-thru at McDonald's and come home in the cherry-red Corvette they saw on the way there, that some other Otter talked them into buying! If you have an Otter in your life, you're definitely in for some fun…and also a few surprises. Otters don't make decisions based on facts; they go with their gut. Sometimes this spontaneous approach to life brings joy and adventure, but sometimes it brings problems.

Otters are the dreamers, always thinking about the future, about the next big thing. They are idea factories, and because they're so verbal, they'll tell you all about themselves. Words like "never" and "always" and "everybody" are common in an Otters' vocabulary because they communicate to express themselves rather than to relay factual information. They are dramatic: lots of highs and lows, wins and losses. The facts and the details are not usually important to them. There's no need to correct their exaggerated stories; just let them communicate with passion. They want the recognition and approval.

TIPS FOR DEALING WITH AN OTTER:
- *Expect an Otter to act like an Otter.* They live a life of adventure, often bouncing from one thing to another and from one person to another. Understand that they are far more interested in people than in tasks. Try not to take it personally.
- *Speak the language of an Otter.* Praise, praise, praise them, and they'll do anything for you. Even if you doubt their ability to follow through, be enthusiastic about their ideas. There are times when it will be challenging to find a balance between sharing their excitement versus worrying that they might make one of those impulsive decisions. These are the times when you'll have to choose your

words carefully because your approval is so important to them. They will need affirmation that you think they're great and that it's just not so sure about this idea.

- *Otters are motivated by fun and praise.* If you want to persuade them, show them how what you are wanting will either be fun or win them social approval.

ADVICE FOR AN OTTER:

Otters, my friends, you would benefit greatly from acquiring the skill of *pausing.* Pause to consider the advice of others before you act, pause to create distance during conflict when you are poised to verbally attack, and pause to be sure that you're not just talking others into doing what it is that you want to do. (Remember: It's okay if they want something different or disagree with you. It doesn't mean that they don't think you're great.) So before you buy the new house, perhaps consider the advice of your brother-in-law who is a contractor, rather than make your decision based solely on curb appeal. Or, when your coworker starts an argument, consider walking away before heatedly slamming her personal life which she has aired in the office. Impulsivity and irresponsibility are not traits that others will praise you for, so pausing and listening are skills that will serve you well with people in the future.

HOW TO APPLY THIS TO YOUR LIFE:

These are listed in the next chapter, which continues with the other two personality types. Once you learn all four, there will be ideas for application.

10

Welcome to the Jungle (cont.)
How to relate to different personalities

"The hardest struggle of all is to be something different from what the average man is." Charles M. Schwab

In the last chapter, we talked about the strengths and the weaknesses of the Lion and the Otter. These two are quick to think and quick to act and are easily identified because of it. If someone has little trouble speaking up or if you think of them as a "talker," they are probably an Otter or a Lion. Our quieter friends, those who tend to watch more and speak less, are the Golden Retriever and Beaver.

GOLDEN RETRIEVERS

Golden Retrievers (Goldens, for short) are loyal, even-tempered, friendly creatures. Have you ever had a dog? If so, you know that they are waiting at the door to greet you, smiling and welcoming, glad to see you every single day. What a perfect picture of these wonderful human beings. The Goldens out there are truly golden. They are supportive, pleasant, conversational, and caring. Though they are people focused, like the Otter, relationships are their *top* priority, and they are much slower to act and speak.

The great thing about Goldens is that they are agreeable. However, they're often too agreeable. They have a tendency to be unassertive, not telling you what they really think or want, or telling you indirectly at best. Their strength is that they are tolerant and patient with others. Yet this can be their weakness as well, since they will often sacrifice self for what others want. For instance, because they don't want to disappoint anyone, Goldens have a difficult time saying "no" to people, leading them to over commit.

When Goldens make decisions, they do so interactively, always first asking others what they think or want. Even if you directly ask a Golden what they want, they are likely to respond, "I don't know, what do you want?" The Golden Retriever really doesn't care what you do or don't do; they are just interested in being with you. Because they are people focused, the task is not of great importance. They are truly happy doing whatever you want most of the time. They will be right there by your side, whichever restaurant you want to eat at, whichever movie you want to watch, wherever you might want to go.

Goldens tend to lack initiative and often procrastinate, usually getting things done at the last minute, or not at all, unless it was important to someone. They are not as interested in doing things as they are in being with people. If someone needs to talk, they will stop whatever they are doing to talk, because the person is more important to them than the task. Because they value their relationships so much, they will give in whenever tension arises. In order to avoid conflict, they often do things they don't want to do to make others happy. Furthermore, you will never even know that they didn't want to do it, because they'll say it's a great idea. They'll say and do anything to recreate peace in the relationship, avoiding anything that rocks the boat.

The ideal world for a Golden is one where they have peace and stability in their relationships. They are very content doing the same things the same way. Since people greatly interest them, they love to watch people, and in large groups, they tend to be the observers, not the center of attention. However, in a one-on-one situation, they make great conversationalists. Goldens will do anything for you. They love to serve, especially if you express your appreciation.

TIPS FOR DEALING WITH GOLDENS:
- *Expect Goldens to be Goldens.* They are most interested in being with the people they love, far more than they are interested in tasks. They will lack initiative and assertiveness at times, preferring to move at a slower pace. Try to be patient; they simply have different values.
- *Speak the language of a Golden.* If you really want to know what a Golden is thinking, you must first make them feel safe. One of their greatest fears is losing stability or losing a relationship. So when conflict or tension arises, assure them that you are okay and that the relationship is fine, but that you just want to deal with the issue at hand.
- *Goldens are motivated by stable relationships.* Appeal to their desire to do things together, to make decisions together, and to live life together, peacefully.

ADVICE FOR A GOLDEN
My Golden friends, your relationships could really benefit from you *initiating* and *speaking up* about what you really want when you

have a preference. Relationships grow deeper as we share more of who we are. So when your friend wants to go to a restaurant that you have absolutely no desire to go to, speak up and let your friend know. Or if you have readily committed to a new project, despite not having the time to complete it, because you fear letting down your coworker, initiate the conversation to let your coworker know you aren't able to commit to the project after all. Conflict, though it seems so unpleasant, can actually lead to greater intimacy and stronger bonds if both parties can find resolution. People are sometimes upset in the heat of the moment, but they will be fine in your relationship again soon. Just give them a minute to get over it, and don't change your mind because they express displeasure.

BEAVERS

Have you ever noticed a beaver out in the woods? If you are walking through the woods and see a deer or a squirrel, it will quickly run away. But if you are walking through the woods and come across a beaver, it won't run. First of all, it might not even notice that you're there, a common complaint of those with Beavers in their lives. But even if that Beaver does see you, he will go right on doing what he was doing: collecting the precise piece of wood to put in the exact place based on their detailed architectural plans for the dam, which include escape routes A, B, C, and G. Yes, D, E, and F were found to be inferior, hence the inclusion of G. The Beaver wants only a top quality dam and takes pride in a job well done. While the Lion will get the dam done and get it done quickly, the Beaver will take three times as long, but it will be the most excellent, perfect dam in the history of dams because nothing less will do.

Beavers think things through, cover every base, and gather every fact to make the best decision and do the best job in the right way—because there is a right way. Now, this thorough, analytical nature does not leave much room for spontaneity and fun. While their excellence brings great value, they can sometimes be killjoys as they tend be overly cautious. Plus, their eye for perfection allows them to pinpoint what is wrong and make it right, but it also gives them a tendency to be critical and pessimistic, as they will often see what is "wrong" with you and tell you what you "should" or "should not" have done.

If you grow impatient with them and conflict occurs, there's a good chance they'll avoid future conflict and possibly even avoid you. While

Goldens are reserved but tend to give in, Beavers are simply reserved without giving in. You will find them with mouths closed and arms crossed when they are stressed or in conflict. You may also find them working out in the garage or in the kitchen, tending to their tasks and avoiding you during these times of conflict. Beavers can be passive-aggressive creatures; they will sometimes let you know they are upset in subtle ways but won't want to deal with the issue directly.

Beavers can be great listeners, and they tend to ask a lot of insightful, analytical questions. But you will have to guard your sensitivity to their criticism. They have a critical eye, and they notice the missing details first, instead of looking at the big picture. Because getting things exactly right is so important to them, they often need time to process; they don't like to be put on the spot. They are slower to speak and act, so expect decisions to take time as they carefully analyze every angle. It's the Beaver who will have visited two dozen websites, read countless articles, and shopped numerous stores before purchasing the $100 vacuum.

TIPS FOR DEALING WITH BEAVERS:
- *Expect Beavers to act like Beavers.* They are slow-paced, task-oriented people who want to do the job well. And because a job well done is so important to them, they greatly dislike being put on the spot, having to make quick decisions, being forced to change their plans, or being interrupted during a task. Try not to take it personally; they simply have different values.
- *Speak the language of a Beaver.* One of their greatest fears is being wrong, which is why they tend to avoid conflict. Because excellence is so important to them, they don't take criticism lightly. Your criticism means not only that they did or said something less than excellent, but that they failed. Further, since tasks are so much a part of who they are, it means that they are a failure. Even suggestions will often be heard as criticism, so you must choose your words extremely carefully around them or learn simply to keep your mouth shut when it isn't particularly important.
- *Beavers are motivated by being right and doing things well.* Their ideal world is one where they have the time to process and perfect those details that are so important to them. Thus, you must patiently give them plenty of time to make decisions. If you want to persuade them, use research, logic, and facts.

ADVICE FOR A BEAVER:

Our Beavers could stand to learn to be more *adaptable* and *flexible*. Every decision in life does not have to be made with absolute certainty. Beavers must learn to consider that there are other ways of doing things despite what they think someone "should" or "should not" do. So when Jerry wants to put the shelf up quickly before the in-laws come over without measuring the wall space, it's okay; allow him to do so. Or when your college-age son drops by and wants to take you out to dinner even after you have already painstakingly taken time to create a well-planned, coordinated dinner, be flexible, drop everything, and spend time with your son! Just because someone prefers to live life differently does not mean that they are doing something wrong.

THE WHOLE TEAM

At the end of the day, despite all our differences, quirks, and weaknesses, we need the whole team for the sake of humanity.

We need Otters to think outside the box, create enthusiasm, get everyone on board, and catapult our future forward. They are probably why humans can fly like birds in the sky in an airplane!

Lions get the job done, hold others accountable, make tough calls, persevere through obstacles right to the end, and aren't afraid to challenge the status quo. They are why genocides end.

Beavers carefully plan, think through the details, cover every base, bring up important questions through their skepticism and critical eye, and keep at a task until it's perfected. They are why we have medicines that cure cancer.

Golden Retrievers keep the peace, encourage others in their darkest moments, and are often the glue of an organization or family. They are why Lions, Otters, and Beavers don't quit jobs, leave families, or make detrimental decisions. Their listening ears play a vital role to calm an angry Lion, empathize with an Otter to keep their creative juices flowing, and allow Beavers to have a safe place to process their thoughts.

Truly, we all need one another. **Rather than focusing on why you can't get along with that person who is so different than you, perhaps identify what makes them so valuable and tap into that strength!**

And may I also suggest that you consider how you interact with that person. You might be unintentionally pushing their buttons. How do you identify the personality type(s) of people in your life? Hopefully these chapters gave you some ideas, but here are a couple scenarios that might ring true for you and prove helpful. These are written to describe what each of the personalities would do and why they would do it. Sometimes personalities look alike because they do some of the same things, but they are doing them for different reasons. For example, an Otter, a Golden, and a Beaver can all procrastinate a task, but for different reasons.

You receive a text message from a friend or family member asking you a question:

- _Lion_ – Quickly and immediately respond using the fewest possible letters. It is quite possible that your text cannot be understood by the recipient. In fact, when later asked, _you_ might not even be able to understand what you wrote.
- _Otter_ – Text back using as many words and emoticons as possible. Continue the conversation by inviting your friend to some event.
- _Golden Retriever_ – Pick up the phone and call them. Be sure to ask how their family is.
- _Beaver_ – When you notice the message, text a short message back, using correct capitalization and punctuation.

At work, you're given a task and instructions on what to do.

- _Lion_ – Identify the most efficient way to complete the task and do it immediately. The instructions were just a suggestion for someone who didn't know what they were doing. Accomplish this along with twenty other things before lunch.
- _Otter_ – Discuss it with your friends at lunch. Express your utter disbelief at the absurdity of it. Or, express your joy at being chosen to do such an important task. Wait until the last minute to actually do it, and when you email it to your supervisor, copy in a few other people if you think you did a good job.
- _Golden Retriever_ – Next time you see the person who assigned the task, ask them how they are doing. You don't even think of the task. If they mention it, ask them what they want to ensure you know how to please them. Procrastinate the task because people are coming to talk with you.

- _Beaver_ – Ask a dozen questions about the task. Be sure to analyze every detail carefully. Express uncertainty about it. If pressed, prioritize the task among your other work. But procrastinate if you don't think you will do it well. Follow the instructions completely, even though you know the "right" way. Triple check your work before submitting.

HOW TO APPLY THIS TO YOUR LIFE:

First things first: have you figured out which animal best represents you? Did you take the free quiz noted at the end of the last chapter? **Which animal are you? What strengths do you have as a _____ (Lion, Otter, Golden, or Beaver)?**

What areas could you work on? Be specific. We all have areas we could definitely grow in. Do you react too quickly (Otter)? Maybe bulldoze people (Lion)? Judge much (Beaver)? Give in too frequently (Golden)?

What motivates you? Write down one example of when this type of motivation worked for you.

Now that you know the different personality types, you are ready to change some things with _that_ person. You know who I'm talking about: that person that you are ready to strangle . . . yeah, that person. **Who do you have the most conflict with? Which animal best represents him/her?**

In hopes of future peaceful conversations with this person, what can _you_ do about it? You actually have quite a bit of power here to make things change. **How can you change to better speak his/her language?** (Refer to "tips" at the end of each personality section.)

Let's say you really want this person to see a situation differently. Or maybe it would be great if he/she would come alongside you in a certain project. **What ways can you motivate this person?** (Refer to "tips" at the end of each personality section.)

Let's say you are trying to make changes and things start looking better for you. I mean, why not? If by making some small changes, you end up reaping major benefits then it's a win-win situation. You speak their language, they feel good about it, and you get what you want! **How will speaking their language and how to motivate them directly benefit *you*?**

Further Reading:
Smalley, Gary Ph.D. and John Trent Ph.D. *The Two Sides of Love*. Carol Stream: Tyndale House, 1990.

11

WAR
Wants, Approach . . . Results!

"Wisdom is the power to see and the inclination to choose the best and highest goal, together with the surest means of attaining it." J. I. Packer

All conflict happens for one single reason: we didn't get something we wanted. Sure, we could talk about what someone should or shouldn't do or who was right and who was wrong. But when we spend our time and energy discussing this, we lose sight of one simple thing: what was it we really wanted in the first place and how can we get it?

Jane wants Steve to be on time. They have been married for over thirty years now, and even on their wedding day Steve was late. Pretty much every day thereafter, he has been late. Everywhere they go as a family, they are late. If they are going to church, they're late. If Steve is supposed to be home for dinner, he's late. I spent a lot of time with this family growing up and can attest that he is almost always late.

It seemed like their entire lives were spent playing out this "late script." Steve would say, "I'll be home at five o'clock," so Jane would have dinner ready by five o'clock. She'd wait ten, fifteen, twenty minutes...no Steve. So Jane starts fuming. She's slamming dishes on the table and throwing silverware around. She wants to know that when he says he'll be home at five, he'll be home at five. Yet he continues to walk in the door after they've eaten, cleaned up dinner, and sometimes gone to bed. The fight ensues. Jane says, "I thought you said you were going to be home at five!" She attacks him, he attacks her right back, and the battle rages until the damage is done and the wounded walk away—not at all what they really wanted in the first place.

I wonder what other approach Jane might have used—because her usual approach certainly did not get the results she wanted. I wonder if she had used the same words, but perhaps forced them to come out softer ("I was expecting you at five, what happened?"), if the discussion might have gone quite differently. Perhaps the war might have been avoided entirely.

The approach we choose has a big impact on the results we get. We could argue all day long about how Steve was dishonest or inconsiderate, how he shouldn't have said he was going to be home at five if he wasn't going to be home at five. We can go back and forth about what someone should or should not do, but that doesn't really end the war, does it? **Determining who is right and who is wrong is useless and even damaging. What we want to determine is the most effective approach.**

Determining who is right and who is wrong is useless and even damaging. What we want to determine is the most effective approach.

When Steve's daughter, Lisa, was growing up, she also battled with her dad over his lateness. Sunday afternoons were designated family time, but Sunday night was youth group, and Lisa loved going to youth group. Youth group started at six o'clock. If they went out during family time, Steve usually had to stop at the office to pick something up or do just "one more thing," and, inevitably, Lisa would be late. Sometimes she didn't even make it to youth group. Lisa would get upset with her dad and used a similar approach to her mother: "You said we'd be home by six, but we weren't home by six! I'm not going anywhere with you anymore!" Then the typical battle ensued.

But it didn't take long for Lisa to realize how things worked. She learned that if told her dad that she had to be home by six, most of the time it wouldn't happen. So Lisa decided to tell her dad not that she *had* to be home by *six*, but that she *wanted* to be home by *three*. If he asked, "Hey, do you want to go with me to do this?" Lisa would say, "I really want to, Dad, but I have youth group, and I really want to be home by three o' clock." He would reassure her, "Oh, three, of course we'll be home by three." Lisa learned that he was not usually late by more than two hours, so she found that allowing a three-hour cushion was usually a safe strategy.

Lisa didn't initially start with that three-hour window of time. She initially started with one hour, requesting that she be home by five o'clock, but they were still never on time for youth group. She then went to four o'clock, which was better, but still there were times that they would not make it home by six. Three o'clock was the magic number. If she told him three, somehow they could make it home by six. By using these different approaches, trial-and-error style, Lisa eventually got the results she was looking for, which were: 1) Lisa wanted to go and do things with her dad, and 2) She wanted to be home in time to go to youth group.

You see, when you think about what you want (e.g. "I want to buy the Porsche"), you have to expand the question to include every aspect of what you want. You want the Porsche, but what *else* do you want? "I want to buy the Porsche, *and* I want my spouse to be happy with the decision, *and* I want to be financially stable, *and* I want my payment to be less than $300 a month, *and...*" Playing this out helps you realize every aspect of what you *really* want and not just what you think you want in the moment. After all, you don't want to buy the Porsche and then regret it because you're broke and your spouse hasn't talked to you for quite a long time.

In my example, Lisa wanted to spend quality time with her dad and be on time for youth group. She accomplished both, and I believe you can usually have both. You can have what you want *and* maintain great relationships. However, there will be times when you realize that what you want is just not worth the cost to the relationship or is not equal to the downfalls that will come with it, such as wanting a Porsche but being unwilling to sacrifice annual family vacations. Maybe you love running, and you're just aching to get out for a nice ten-mile run. But Wednesday night is the prime opportunity for family time in your week, and it's just not worth it, so you run three miles instead. There are likely other ways or other days to get your running fix, but because family comes before running for you, Wednesday is not the best time to run for 2 hours.

There are other times when the cost to the relationship might be minor enough that you still choose to move forward with your choice, even though the other person might disagree. Sometimes a loved one will be upset in the moment, but in the long term, the results of your choice will benefit them (e.g. a man chooses to do poker nights once a month knowing that it helps him de-stress, which is better for both him and his family). Be careful and judicious when making these kinds of decisions that sacrifice one want for another, since most of the time you can have *both* what you want and peace in your relationships. The point is that you should take the time to first think through all of what you *really* want. There might be a good, a greater good, and a greatest good that you value more than the immediate want in front of you. For example, our husband who chooses to do poker nights, knowing it helps him de-stress, might also decide to host poker night at his house, so that he is home with the kids while his wife gets a night out. Thus, he gets time to de-stress *and* she does as well.

Once you realize every aspect of what you want, you must be willing to try different approaches to get the results you're looking for. While Lisa could have just given up and said, "Forget it! I'm not going with you, Dad, because you're never on time!" that wouldn't have gotten her what she really wanted – time with Dad *and* time at youth group. Think about it in terms of winning the WAR:

> **W**ants
>
> **A**pproach
>
> **R**esults

Ask yourself, "Is what I'm doing now (i.e. your **A**pproach) getting me the **R**esults that I **W**ant?" **If your approach isn't working out for you, it's not a matter of blaming the other person for being so horrible; rather, it's a matter of finding the approach that will be most likely to succeed in getting you results.**

> *If your approach isn't working out for you, it's a matter of finding the approach that will be most likely to succeed in getting you results.*

Molly had a problem. As the administrative assistant, it was her job to process her coworkers' travel vouchers, which were continually scattered across the office. Molly's desk was in a room with all the copiers and filing cabinets, and when people came in to perform other tasks, they would just leave their vouchers in various places—everywhere except the folder where they belonged. Molly found herself scouring the office every month to find them and ensure they were all paid. It sometimes took her forty-five minutes to locate all of them, and occasionally she would miss one, only to be faced with an angry coworker who hadn't been reimbursed.

Molly felt that this time-consuming task was taking away from more important work and decided that she wanted it to stop. She wanted to be able to go to the folder and process the vouchers, *and* she wanted her coworkers to be paid on time so that there would be harmony in their relationships (Wants). So Molly started a new system. She politely informed everyone that she would be happy to process any travel voucher she found in the appropriate folder, apologizing for how vouchers had been late in the past and reassuring everyone that this new system would ensure timely payment. She kindly informed them where the new folder was, which was now bright red to avoid any confusion (Approach). The first month, half of her coworkers did not get their vouchers processed on time because they had failed to place them in the folder. For each complaint, Molly politely apologized and offered compassion, but kept her resolve and shared the solution: "I'm so sorry it didn't get paid out. I hate for you to be out that money. I processed all the ones in the red folder. I wonder what happened?" Each time, the coworker rather unhappily admitted their mistake, to which she replied with genuine kindness, "Don't worry—next time it will be in there, and it will be sure to get processed." By the third month, every voucher made its way to the red folder and her coworkers were paid on time (Results).

My kids (Shannon) used to gripe at each other on the way to school in the morning. It was usually something little, like "You're on my side of the car," "Why can't you move your backback!" or "Caden forgot to turn the light out in the bathroom." What I *wanted* wasn't just for my kiddos to stop arguing on the way to school, but more importantly, I wanted them to be on each other's side. Life is hard enough without your family members being hard on you too. I wanted them to be supportive of each other. That's not asking too much, is it? So I tried the lecturing route: "You guys should be thankful for each other..." Nope. That didn't do it. I tried the threatening route: "If you guys can't treat each other kindly, then I'm..." Nope, not that either. Okay. Think. Think. Think. What could work for *my* kids? Ah-ha! We now do three things every day on the way to school, and honestly, this approach totally changed the relationship my kids have with one another. I got the result I wanted! Every day on the way to school we pray together out loud, and then I have my kids say one thing to encourage each other (e.g. "Good luck on your test today!"). They also ask each other about the day ahead, so that they know how to best encourage. Bonus! Then, as they head off to class, they either give each other high fives or fist bumps. It's now our second year doing this. I am so glad I left the lecturing and threatening behind! It wasn't working for anyone. **Changing our approach changed our results.**

> *Changing our approach changed our results.*

HOW TO APPLY THIS TO YOUR LIFE:

So what is it that you really want? Do you actually want your mother-in-law to stop giving you advice? Or is it just that you want some boundaries as to when she gives advice and on what subjects? What will it cost the relationship? Your approach **will** matter. So what do you want?

Think about that want from all angles. Ask yourself, "Is this the only thing I want, or is there something else that goes along with it?" (Think back to Lisa's wants—to both spend time with her dad and be on time for youth group.) **What else do you want?**

If you recall, in Shannon's story about her kids, the first two approaches to "make" them treat each other kindly both failed miserably. The third approach was the winner. Play out in your mind how you think an approach will work, so that you can choose effective ones. You also want to choose approaches that you are 90% sure you will actually do. **Write down three approaches you will try to get what you want.**

You will have to come back to this question after you've tried each approach (unless you get what you want from the first one!), so remind yourself to write out the results from each approach. Perhaps program a reminder into your phone, put sticky notes on your mirror, or email yourself . . . **What were the results from your approaches?** Which approach got you what you wanted? Or is it back to the drawing board to figure out different approaches?

12

Little Devil
Feeding our good side and starving the bad

"Life consists in what a man is thinking all day long." Ralph Waldo Emerson

It was not one of my better moments in life.

A few months before my daughter graduated from nursing school, I spoke to her about some car troubles she was having. She needed to change the spark plugs, and I directed her to a friend in town who would fix it all for free. I fully expected that by graduation, when we were to move all of her stuff from Illinois to Georgia that the car would be in good working order.

Just after the graduation ceremony, I drove her car to the hotel to pick her up and say goodbye to family before heading out, but the car could not even go 20 mph because the engine had no power. At this point, it was no longer a few bucks for spark plugs but thousands of dollars for a new engine. There was no way this car was going to make it 12 more hours through the Smoky Mountains to Georgia.

As I drove to the hotel, there was a classic angel-devil conversation going on in my head. You know how in old cartoons there is a little angel on one shoulder and a little devil on the other, each trying to influence the decision. Now the little devil had a lot of credibility in this situation because this was my daughter's *fifth* car and she was only 20 years old. While not all of the cars died because of her mistakes, she did seem to have considerable difficulty attending to those little flashing lights on her dashboard. If this had been the first occasion, the little angel might have had a stronger leg to stand on, but at that moment, the devil was ready to *kill* her. I'm guessing you have little angels and devils whispering in your ears too.

The little devil was loud and clear: "I cannot believe she did not take this stupid car to get fixed for $14!" Then the angel sweetly reminded me, "It's graduation weekend. Stuff doesn't matter; people matter. Just roll with it." The little angel was winning, so I called ahead to explain the situation to my husband and told him we would need to redistribute all of her possessions from this car to another because this car was *not* going to Georgia. I arrived at the hotel after much deep breathing and pulled up alongside our truck to allow some of her stuff to be transferred into it. My daughter joined me in the parking lot and began pouring oil into her engine with the full intention of driving the car to Georgia.

My first responses were actually sane. I explained to her how danger-ous this was, describing the road and the lack of compression in her car. However, this only lasted a few moments, since she did not appear to be complying. I got louder and louder; soon my hands were flailing, and before too long, plug your ears because my language was now loud and colorful. (This is when you know you've gone over the edge!)

I quickly locked my little angel in the closet and began screaming at the top of my lungs. Fear was driving me to new levels. While my daughter was saying things like, "I'm a grown woman. You need to let me make my own decisions. This is my car, and I'm driving it to Georgia!" I was envisioning her driving right off the Smoky Mountains and plummeting to her death. I was completely over the edge, but the best part was that everyone could see: in-laws, cousins, aunts, uncles. *Everyone* had the opportunity to watch from their hotel rooms which happened to face the parking lot. Not to mention the scene was difficult to ignore at our loud volume.

There came a point when I decided to ignore the fruitless conversation and simply take the keys from her and begin transferring cargo over to our truck and my mother-in-law's car. Needless to say, we were both stewing. This is what we do when these moments are over, right? We stew. She's stewing. I'm stewing.

And what do we do to unload our pent up anger? We look for a listening ear. So, I called someone. And who did I call? When I'm stewing, I don't call a friend who will tell me to be the bigger person, who will remind me to be the parent, not the child. No, I went back into the hotel room and called one of those good friends who would attempt to be supportive but would just end up fueling the little devil.

I wonder if we make these calls because we feel guilty about how poorly we've just acted. **We know deep down that, despite what the other person did or did not do, our response only made things worse.** So now I had anxiety, not only from the fear of my daughter driving off a cliff, but from how poorly I be-haved. And so, like any good friend, my friend "helped" me feel better with phrases like: "You couldn't have let her go. You were just protect-ing her." It's not that these statements aren't true. It's just that there are better ways I could have handled it, aren't there? Instead of helping me to

> *We know deep down that, despite what the other person did or did not do, our response only made things worse.*

be the bigger person, my phone call had made things worse. With my friend's support, I felt justified and did nothing to make the situation better. Instead of finding a way to move forward, I felt righteous in doing what I did.

Luckily, while the little devil continued ranting and raving in my head with his megaphone, my mother-in-law was the still, small voice of the angel. When she hugged me goodbye, she said, "Don't kill her." Then she looked me square in the eye and encouraged me to calm down rather than continue in my fury. Immediately, the little angel and little devil began their battle again.

The one that I feed the most is the one that is going to win. When we call people who feed the little devil, we are very unproductive. We make things worse in our relationships instead of better. So, in moments like these, I need to feed my angel and starve my devil because I know the angel will help me make good decisions. I must refuse to let the little devil repeat his lines in my head and to others. I have to shut him up and listen to the angel. Easier said than done! We all have this little devil, though yours might sound a bit different from mine. Knowing those lines he repeats in our heads and **learning to recognize the voice of our little devil will ultimately help us ignore him**.

The book, *Crucial Conversations*, lists three voices: the victim, the villain, and the helpless.[8] These are three voices that the little devil tends to take; which voice do you hear most often?

- The victim says, "Look at what they did to me."
- The villain says, "He's such a jerk!" or "She *knows* I hate that!"
- The helpless voice says, "There's nothing I can do" or "I've tried everything."

The first two voices are ways of blaming others for our problems and the third voice makes us feel weak and at the mercy of our problems. All of them steal our power to make good, healthy relational decisions. These voices are destructive to us and to our relationships.

Listening to any of these voices is like listening to only half a story. We must be intentional about telling the whole story.

- If you listen to the victim voice, the other half of the story involves acknowledging your role in the situation and taking responsibility for it.

- If you listen to the villain voice, the other half of the story involves removing the negatively skewed filter through which you see the world and humanizing all those people you've turned into villains in your head.
- If you listen to the helpless voice, you're missing the other half of the story that involves your underused resources, power, and creativity—you *are* able to do *something* about this!

One of the quickest ways to get these voices to quiet down is to find someone to feed our little angel side, someone we can call who helps us to be the bigger person and have the best in our relationships. We often don't like to talk to these people because they "don't understand" and they tell us things we don't want to hear. If you don't already have one of these people, you might need to start forming some new relationships.

> *One of the quickest ways to get these voices to quiet down is to find someone to feed our little angel side...*

Every time I move, I find another mentor. My rule for a mentor is that she has to be older than my mother. Think back to when you were younger: you can clearly see your mistakes now, but they made so much sense to you at the time. As we get older, we see the past with more clarity and we chalk up life experience and wisdom for the future. **So find someone who has already covered the road ahead of you.** Good mentors are hard to find. I have moved nine times in 18 years, so I'm always looking for my next mentor. Sometimes I find a woman who is a great mentor for parenting issues, but maybe not so great for my marriage. Perhaps another woman is really great at career mentoring, but would not be a good candidate for mentoring me about my finances.

There are times we might need professionals, but we also need a support network in our lives that we can tap into on a regular basis. We need a variety of mentors because we have a variety of roles and issues that we face. For some, the thought of forming new relationships seems tough, but these relationships can be life changing and the key to leading you toward the kind of relationships and life you would relish. You don't have to make any commitment when looking for a mentor; just start by making plans for coffee, lunch, or a walk through the neighborhood.

As a side note, I recommend your mentor be a person of the same gender. Even though you may think you have no romantic interest, opposite gender relationships are not worth the potential danger if you or they are married. Nobody walks into a room, takes off all their clothes, and says, "Oops, I committed adultery!" Most people have affairs with coworkers and close friends, not random strangers, because our proximity with that person naturally creates intimacy. You don't know how many times I've had people in my counseling office tell me that they had zero attraction to the person initially, that sometimes the person was even decades older, but they still ended up having an affair. Most of these people told me they always thought they would "never" have an affair. Be wise: find a mentor of your gender.

We also have people in our lives who feed the dark side of us, who give that little devil a megaphone. Ultimately, they stir us up instead of helping us think clearly and wisely. Sometimes it's wise to end relationships with these people altogether. However, sometimes they are permanent in our lives because they happen to be related to us or work in our cubicle. With these people, we may have to make certain topics off limits and say to ourselves, "With Fred, I will no longer talk about my boss, because when I talk about my boss with him, it makes things worse rather than better." You may need to make your marriage, your kids, or your coworkers off limits in conversations with these people. You will have to be very intentional because they probably enjoy these particular conversations. So when your sister asks, "So, how's it going with Joe?" you will need to be ready with an answer: "You know, Joe and I are working on things. So are you going to the game tomorrow night?" Be prepared to avoid getting sucked back into that conversation.

Ultimately, I'm always on the hunt for the people who feed my little angel and nudge me a little closer to being a better person and having better relationships.

HOW TO APPLY THIS TO YOUR LIFE:

What are the favorite sayings of your little devil? Do you hear the victim, the villain, or the helpless voice most often? Some of us hear the same voice for everyone, but others have different voices that we hear for different people. For my mother, I hear: "She knows I hate that!" For my spouse: "He never helps out!" For my boss: "There's nothing I can do!" Let these be the cues to remind you to feed your little angel. Write down your little devil's phrases.

Who do you call that feeds your devil? You may have different people for different issues. You may talk to a coworker to complain about your boss, but your sister to complain about your spouse. Commit to ending these types of conversations. Make your boss, your spouse, or whoever you complain about, an off-limits topic. You can do this without them even knowing it.

Be ready with a phrase that you repeat like a broken record whenever you are asked about that person. For example, When <u>Marsha</u> asks about my marriage my broken record phrase is: "<u>We're working on it and getting better.</u>" Or if <u>Fred</u> brings up my boss, my broken record phrase is: "<u>I hear you, but nobody's perfect. I sure wouldn't want his job!</u>" These are lines you can use whenever the subject arises, then change the subject. What lines will you use?

- Person:_____ Broken record phrase:_____
- Person:_____ Broken record phrase:_____
- Person:_____ Broken record phrase:_____

Be ready to change the subject whenever the old conversations arise by finding other topics these people are interested in. For example, when <u>Mary</u> asks about my spouse, I change the topic to <u>her grandkids</u> because she loves to talk about them. What topics will work for you?

- Person:_____ Change topic to:_____
- Person:_____ Change topic to:_____
- Person:_____ Change topic to:_____

Who can feed your little angel side? Maybe there are different people for different relationships. For example, my angel for <u>my daughter</u> is <u>my mother-in-law</u>. But my angel for <u>my spouse</u> is <u>my friend, Cindy</u>. Who can help redirect you to be the bigger person and do the wise and loving thing?

- My angel for _____ is:_____
- My angel for _____ is:_____
- My angel for _____ is:_____

13

The Dance
Overcoming patterns of conflict

"Don't do something permanently stupid because you are temporarily upset." Unknown

Nathan ran to his room crying. Tears fell down his little eight-year-old face. The scene had unfolded so quickly that his mom could only stand there in shock. Her baby was degraded, demoralized, crushed. It was difficult to watch. She hated the pain that he must be feeling, especially since it was caused by his own father! Ultimately, she knew Nathan's father loved him deeply. She knew that he wanted Nathan to grow up to be a good man who was kind and conscientious.

Nathan had not meant to break the lamp, but then again, he never meant to do any of the destructive things he inevitably ended up doing. He was a typical rough-housing little boy who had no thought of the impact of his actions—typical for most eight year olds, but unacceptable according to his father. Nathan needed to learn to think of others and be courteous of other people's possessions. He had been told repeatedly not to the throw the ball in the house, one item on a long list of activities that were only to be done outside. This time, Dad decided on a new tactic and spoke with loud, harsh tones to get his point across.

Thus, the fight between mom and dad began. It was nothing new. As parents, they had replayed this one at least a hundred times. This was their "kid script." They had five scripts: the house script, the money script, the sex script, the garbage script, and the kid script. Once again they went round and round until Dad ended up leaving and Mom went to bed angry.

Mom was trying to "help." That's what we do, isn't it? We like to "help" people, don't we? We really do need to put on our rose-colored glasses because most people do not intend to be malicious, they mean to be helpful. When she approached her husband, she did not intend to be cruel, unkind, or demeaning. She really just wanted to make things better for him and Nathan. She thought she could help. She was trying to say, "You don't know how you're coming across." But her delivery didn't work. We want to look for what works. We all have our moments; there are moments when our delivery might really stink, and there are moments when their delivery might really stink. But we don't usually intend to be malicious or cruel. Usually we are trying to do something that's probably a pretty good thing; it just doesn't come across that way.

The wife says, "You're too hard on him," and the dance begins. Let's speculate for a minute. When she says these words, how do you think the husband feels? He might feel disrespected and misunderstood. Now, when he feels this way, how do you think he might respond? There are three basic responses humans have when they feel threatened: fight, flight, or freeze. Let's say he's a fighter. So he might escalate and start rationalizing his actions. But what did he *really* want? He probably wanted validation and support. But escalation and rationalization do not get him validation and support. And yet this will continue to be his side of the dance every single time, unless he chooses to learn new dance steps.

The incoming words "You're too hard on him" trigger a knee-jerk reaction. He feels disrespected and misunderstood, and his knee-jerk reaction is to escalate and rationalize. Now, when he escalates, how do you think it makes her feel? I'm guessing she probably feels misunderstood and inadequate. Like him, when these threatening feelings arise, she has a knee-jerk reaction of fight, flight, or freeze. Let's say she a fighter and she stonewalls and belittles in response. What happens when she belittles him? Once again, he feels misunderstood, so he escalates more. She then feels even more inadequate and freezes, so she begins stonewalling, so he feels more disrespected, and on and on it goes. This is how we start with "You're too hard on him" and end with "I'm done—it's over!" This is how it works, isn't it? It happens to us too, doesn't it? We get sucked into this crazy dance, hurling hurt all over each other.

At the end of the day, whatever happened to make her say, "You're too hard on him," probably wasn't all that significant. He yelled at his son; that's not the end of the world. Who hasn't done that? We all have our moments. And it's in those moments that the dance begins, turning something small into an avalanche that destroys our relationships, leaving us cold and distant.

We all have emotional knee-jerk reactions that we use to defend ourselves when we're hurting. I personally react with escalation—not one of my finer points. These reactions are just the symptoms of someone hurting. We are all wired differently, so we each use our own reactions when emotion hits us. He reacts with escalation; she reacts with stonewalling. We also tend to expect others to react differently, which usually means we want them to validate and listen to us, not react defensively toward us. We say, "Quit yelling at me," only to get, "Well, you quit belittling me." But we cannot choose what their knee-jerk reactions are, and we all have knee-jerk reactions that are unproductive and hurtful.

But we look at others and say, "I would never do that," which is probably true. Your knee-jerk reactions are different. Maybe you would never yell, but you might belittle. And if I asked you to stop doing that, it would be tough for you. Have you ever tried to change a bad habit? Is there anything you've done for years, something you hate about yourself but can't seem to overcome no matter how hard you try?

I have something like this. I speak in commands. I don't ask you for help ("Would you please hand me that?"). Instead, I tell: "Hand me that." This is not the most polite way of speaking. It is viewed as rude and offensive by many people. But, even after decades of trying to be more polite, I still resort to my default mode and tell people what to do instead of asking them. I do not mean to be rude or disrespectful. It's not my intention, but it happens. Likewise, the wife didn't mean to attack or judge, but the way she spoke just didn't work. We have to learn a new way to relate to one another. It's a little like learning a foreign language. It's difficult to know what words are best or even to remember any words at all. For me, making requests is not my native language. My thoughts automatically form into commands, not requests. So it takes a lot of awareness and hard work to reform my thoughts into requests and speak this new language of politeness to others.

We see these default modes originate at an early age, hardwired into the brain. Though environmental, social, and spiritual influences do impact us, there's some biology at work here too. Just try to tie the shoes of any two-year-old. One child will announce that she can tie them without your help, insisting, "Me do it!" Now, did she learn that from her parents? Maybe. But I have friends who are the most passive, gentle people in the world, and their daughter says, "Me do it!" I assure you, she did not learn that from them. Even when I try to read her a story, she takes the book and says, "Me read to you." She points to the words and tells me which words to read. She is very directive, very instructional. She's going to be a great little CEO one day, if her parents don't kill her first.

But if you take my two-year-old cousin and try to tie her shoes, she just kicks back and says, "Thanks, you the best!" She has no interest in tying her own shoes. But she's a charmer! You see, this is the wiring in our brains. These children grow into adults, and they don't mean to be rude and bossy or charming and manipulative. But relationships with both a "Me do it!"

paired with a "Thanks, you're the best! You go ahead and do it all" can get hairy!

Have you ever been to a foreign country where you didn't speak the language? What do we do? We use our nonverbals and try to translate their meaning. Because we don't know the language, we don't rely as much on the words. Instead, we focus on other cues to understand them. These are the real skills that we want to learn today: how to communicate well with more than just our words and also how to translate in the foreign lands of our friends and family. When those we love speak with their knee-jerk reactions, we need to learn to listen for their hurt and translate appropriately, so that we don't end up dancing like the couple earlier in this chapter. Who wants to dance like that anyway? It's so painful for us all. We have to learn a new way to speak and translate to get out of the dance.

While I was serving as an Air Force Chaplain, I was sent to Turkey. I did not speak Turkish but wanted to pick up some key phrases. The first things I wanted to learn were "please" and "thank you." I remember that as a child, I couldn't get anything without using these "magic words." We teach these to our two-year-olds because in our country we value politeness. Yet as adults, we forget these simple tools. How do you get what you want? You have to ask nicely.

Therefore, while in Turkey, the first thing I needed to learn was how to be courteous. Lutfen, which means please, was going to be crucial during my time there. Even if I butchered the rest of their language, I could always throw out a "lutfen," and I would get a lot further. People are typically kind and courteous. Add to this the nonverbal cues of smiling or softly touching a forearm or shoulder, and you can say a whole lot to the other person, even when you don't yet know a word of their language. We can do this! We just forget how in our adult relationships. Instead, our nonverbals reflect our hurt, which only leads to more hurt. But, in the same way, showing love leads to more love. **If all else fails, there are universal nonverbal ways of saying, "I care about you, and this is going to be okay." These types of responses can get you out of the dance quickly.**

> *If all else fails, there are universal nonverbal ways of saying, "I care about you, and this is going to be okay." These types of responses can get you out of the dance quickly.*

Now, it might not get you out of the first round. If someone gets extremely upset, then "I'm so sorry, honey" likely won't work the first time. You might get a response of "You're darn right—you better be sorry!" But as long as you stop following your knee-jerk reactions of belittling or escalating, and instead speak the language of love and gentleness, you can end this. We want to end this. Our emotions may be high, and our adrenaline may be pumping, ready for a fight, but we can calm down and be a soothing presence, helping the other person sense the respect and validation that they want.

What did the wife in our illustration want? She probably wanted to be understood. How well did her reactions of stonewalling and belittling create understanding? How well do your reactions get you what you really want? They usually do not do this very well. We have to develop new skills because our current ones keep us dancing, which hurts us all—and nobody wants that. Even though the wife feels misunderstood and invalidated, what if she chooses *not* to respond with her knee-jerk reactions? What if she responds with love instead?

I have great news! **It only takes one person to stop the dance.** If the wife stops reacting, the entire dance stops. It only takes one to tango! It only takes *one* to end this mess and turn it into something great. You can stop the tango. You can get the understanding and validation you are looking for by learning how to speak their language and translating their knee-jerk reactions as symptoms of hurting people who feel threatened. Once we make ourselves less threatening, they will calm down, and we can then move forward. **When we learn how to translate their responses as pain and respond in ways that help them feel safe and loved, we have amazing relationships. And it only takes one of us to do this!** Sound too simple? The application section can help bring things together.

> *It only takes one person to stop the dance.*

HOW TO APPLY THIS TO YOUR LIFE:

Think of a recent conflict. Imagine yourself back in that conflict and answer the following questions:

What did you feel? Underline all that apply: abandoned, betrayed, controlled, deceived, defective, disconnected, disrespected, like a failure, helpless, humiliated, ignored, inadequate, invalidated, judged, misunderstood, not good enough, rejected, taken advantage of, unimportant, unwanted

List the top three you underlined here:
These are your buttons.

How did you react? Underline all that apply: deny responsibility, blame circumstances or someone else, belittle (call names, mock, or ridicule), catastrophize (exaggerate or dramatize), control, criticize, cross-complain (bring up another issue), defensiveness, demand, dishonesty, escalate (get louder and louder), fact find (usually to prove your point), fix-it mode, humor/sarcasm, invalidate or minimize, isolate yourself (shut down), lecture, mind read (assume intent), pacify (try to calm the other), passive aggressive behavior, rationalize, repeat yourself, rewrite history (view the past as negative), replay the argument in your mind, argue about who is right/wrong, self-deprecate, stonewall, withhold (affection, information, etc.)

List the top three you underlined here:
These are your knee-jerk reactions.

What did you want? Underline all that apply: acceptance, approval, adequate, appreciated, important, loved, peace, respected, safe, supported, trusted, understood, useful, validated, connected, intimate, noticed, competent, good enough, worthwhile

List the top three you underlined here:
These are your goals.

How well did your reactions reach your goals?

What can you do differently the next time your buttons are pushed? **What new responses could replace your reactions so that you can reach your goals?**

Further reading: (The concept of this chapter along with the questions were derived from this book.)

Smalley, Gary, et al. *The DNA of Relationships*. Carol Stream: Tyndale House, 2004.

14

ICU
Just when you think it's over, it's not...

"When we are no longer able to change a situation, we are challenged to change ourselves." Viktor Frankl

I remember the night clearly. I was in the kitchen while Zack was making a snack. We were talking when my phone rang in the other room. I ignored it. A few minutes later, it rang again. Typically, I would have ignored it yet again, but something led me to take the call. When I answered, a concerned but matter-of-fact voice explained that my daughter, Joy, had been in a car accident and was being transported by helicopter to the hospital. While I scrambled to find my shoes and run out the door with my family, I listened to the voicemail that the first caller had left. It was from the paramedic who had arrived at the scene of Joy's accident. He explained that they had just spent 30 minutes trying to pry apart her car enough to carefully remove my daughter's broken body. The prognosis was unknown. Panic gripped me.

When I arrived at the hospital and asked for Joy by name, I was told that she wasn't there and that a social worker was coming to meet with me. I practically fell to the floor. As someone who has visited hospitals regularly, I know why names are not put into the computer. You don't list dead patients. Social workers often serve to provide support and resources for a family during times like this, after the loss of a child. Words cannot explain the devastation I felt.

Loss is always difficult, isn't it? Intense emotion floods us when we experience loss. And loss comes in many shapes and sizes: the death of a child, but also the death of a job, a marriage, or a dream. We don't know what to do in these moments, and in the grip of emotion, we often crash and burn. I see this all the time in my counseling office, especially with the death of a relationship. The death of a relationship usually sounds like "I want a divorce" or "I'm selling my portion of the company." When the message comes, panic grips us. But, as with my call from the paramedic and my exchange with the hospital receptionist, it's not the end of the story. It can seem like it. People often seem completely resolute when they tell us these things, but they may still change their minds, and we can still make an impact on them.

When the social worker came, she took me to Joy. I was not expecting this. I was convinced that she was dead. I was convinced about a lot of things over the days ahead, few of which were good, and most of which were wrong. My daughter Joy is alive and well. She is almost back to 100%, though as I write this it was just three months ago she was broken from head to toe.

What do we do when faced with awful news? First of all, realize that just because it seems to be over, it doesn't have to be. I have seen many a spouse walk out, only to later return and reunite to create an amazing marriage. I have seen bleak, disastrous situations involving prison, drugs, and job loss turn around just when you least expect it. But in any relationship crisis, our response is crucial.

While Joy was in the Intensive Care Unit (ICU) of the hospital, I had one disposition: a positive, hopeful, pleasant one...at least that's what Joy would have thought. No matter what I felt, I was determined to be positive and pleasant in my interactions with her. I reframed all information from the doctor with great enthusiasm and hopefulness. I praised the staff for their care every time they entered the room, even though I may have cussed them out and threatened their lives only moments before in the hallway. All Joy knew was a peaceful, gentle, happy place. She was in the ICU. She was in a very fragile state, and she didn't need to deal with anything else. Her care was not up to my standards, but it would not have been wise to share this with her. Her recovery was quicker this way.

This applies to most relationship crises. Even if this person is repeatedly telling you, "I'm done," if you can stay the course and remain positive in the moments you share with them, it will pay huge returns to move your relationship back in the right direction. On the other hand, we seal our own fate when we act on their declaration of "I'm done" as if it were gospel. The key is to treat them like they are in the ICU. Give the crisis response of compassion and understanding with a shred of hope at the end: "I can understand why you would feel that way. I know these seasons are tough and seem like they won't end" or "I know you're hurting right now. This is a painful phase of life." These subtle statements help the patient reframe without being too threatening. You need to make plans for what may happen, but you also need to keep a positive face and hopeful spirit in your relationship despite the feelings and fears you face.

I was coping with a myriad of feelings, fears, and exhaustion during this time. Joy wanted me there every minute—her momma, not someone else. And I didn't want to leave her alone. I slept on concrete floors, if you could call it sleep. Hospital staff came in and out every hour or two. I had to take care of myself some, both in order to keep myself from cracking and falling apart and in order to be able to support Joy. When I did venture home, I called in back-up to ensure that she was cared for. I still had to make sure I was taken care of, but definitely not by her. She would never have known. This is what you do for people in the ICU, people like your partner, your teenager, or your spouse. Do you have someone who's in the ICU right now?

Luckily, this place doesn't last forever. It is only temporary, though it gets quite tiring and often lasts longer than we want. You'll crack from time to time, maybe even multiple times a day. There are a number of things you have to do for yourself so you can keep up your hopeful spirit. You need sleep. We often have sleepless nights during these times of life, but most of us are grumpy when we don't sleep and allow emotion rather than wisdom to control us. So figure out how to get some sleep. You also need a coach and some cheerleaders. Choose them very, very carefully and shut off all other discussion with anyone else. The seeds of ill-placed words take root quickly and grow like thick weeds to crowd out any seedlings of hope you have. So get a few cheerleaders whom you can call when you want to give up, people who will get you back in the game. Get a coach who can help you brainstorm and plan, who will hold you accountable and constantly refine your strategy. You're going to need all the help you can get because this isn't a random football game, this is the Super Bowl championship—and it is a trophy that will give you joy for the rest of your life. Just be careful who you choose to listen to during this season. The key is to act quickly and strategically; it is a critical time.

THE TALK

Like Joy, your injured partner needs a peaceful place. Simple things that would normally be no big deal, such as passing comments and conversations, are not usually wise for the ICU. **Your injured partner cannot handle your emotion, unless it is positive. He cannot handle your needs.** These are like the broken bones: the slightest movement can cause great pain. **And the most important rule is that you cannot have conversations about the relationship.** *This is likely the very thing you want the most— to know that the commitment is solid.* But you must remain positive. A relationship conversation is damaging and too much to handle right now. Just remember: the ICU does not last forever.

> And the most important rule is that you cannot have conversations about the relationship.

How will you know when it's okay to talk about your relationship? The third time they bring it up. Strange answer, huh? The first few times, we must tread lightly. Like in the ICU, we follow the patient's lead and do what the patient wants. If they are silent, we are silent; if they talk about a topic, we listen quietly and inquire just enough to keep them talking, if they want. If they bring up the relationship, the first few times you should listen and respond, *remembering that this is a patient in the ICU.* Don't think that the patient is recovered just because you experienced a few good times. That is a novice mistake. I've known many couples or business partners in crisis situations who had a good day or a good week and thought it was safe to talk about the relationship. But as soon as they began that conversation, the other person responded in anger or distanced themselves, and then those good moments faded away.

The first two times they initiate a conversation about the relationship or the situation at hand, you are only a mirror. You reflect back whatever they say. If they mention their fears and concerns, you do *not* explain your side, defend your position, or list reasons and justifications. You spend 90% of the time simply agreeing and affirming: "I can understand why you pulled back," or "Who wouldn't be afraid when someone acted like I did?" etc. You might, in some circumstances, share information if there is something important that is inaccurate. If he thought you were at a hotel when you were in fact at a meeting, it would be important information to clarify. But it should never be more than 10% of the conversation. Do not repeat the information. You mention it once and return to agreeing and affirming. You do not have to agree with their views or their conclusion. You are agreeing with their emotion: "I can understand why you would be angry. If I thought I was being lied to, I would be upset too." When you make these statements, you are not saying that you *were* lying. You are only saying that *if* there was lying, you would also be upset. This allows them to drain emotion (see the chapter on "Life Jackets").

You can always share your heart later. You can always bring up your relationship and sort through it once a few positive *months* have passed and the coast is perfectly clear. You do not want to make the mistake of sharing your heart too soon. Relish the moments when the patient is moving back and reconnecting. But even if they lay out the emotions of their heart, and *even if they ask to talk about it*, keep the ICU stance: positive, peaceful, pleasant.

Keep in mind that the ICU patient doesn't know what he is doing. He is in one mode all the time: self-protection. He has decided to crawl behind the Great Wall and hide. His words may even sound cool and calm on the surface, but they conceal an undercurrent of emotion, like the hidden flipping feet of a duck that sails smoothly across the lake. We have all been there. We have all said things we did not mean. Sometimes we even think that we mean them. But that's not the end of the story, it's only a chapter. It's the same here. Despite what the patient is saying, this is only a chapter. It's a sad and painful chapter, one that you would like to end quickly, but I have read this chapter before, and I can tell you that for many it is not the end, even though they say it is.

Furthermore, some come out from behind the Great Wall and never have "the conversation." As humans, we want answers! We want to know *why*. We're afraid it will happen again. But we must resist the urge to insist they tell us "why" because it's very likely that they themselves have no idea. Or they might say it was because of something small, not realizing that the something small was just the final straw. Months down the road, after things return to normal, you may ask "why," to keep the relationship break from happening again. But for most people these answers become less important over time. Only ask if you are truly ready to accept "I don't know" as an answer or to hear an answer that seems unclear or insignificant. If you can fully accept these answers with love and tenderness and without pushing for a better explanation, then you're ready to ask. But more often than not, we push someone right back behind the Great Wall by forcing this conversation on them. Seriously consider this risk and decide if it's really worth it to you. (See the "But Why?!" chapter for more ideas.)

THE LETTER

There are some positive, peaceful things you *can* say, such as writing a letter of apology or acknowledgement for things you know have hurt them. But there are a few rules:

1. Write it down, don't talk about it. Let them know in the letter that you wanted to say it, but didn't want to make them uncomfortable.
2. Make sure you do not share your side of the story or communicate in any defensive manner, thus laying the burden of your emotion on them. It has to be completely about owning your own mistakes and accepting blame and responsibility.
3. Mention any action you have taken to improve. Do not mention things

you plan on doing. Chances are the person has heard you make promises in the past that you have not kept. You can only report what you have already done, not make another promise she probably won't expect you to keep anyway.

4. Acknowledge that they may not be able to forgive you or choose to reconcile and that you can understand why.

5. Let them know you do not expect a response. You owed this to them long ago.

6. Have someone who is older and wiser read your letter, along with these instructions, to ensure you don't break any of these rules. The goal is to validate their feelings, not to state your case, but this can be hard to avoid, so you need an objective proofreader.

7. Only send emotionally charged letters once or twice—once to apologize and again only if something very significant arises that needs clarified or apologized for again (such as if he discovers your affair or you owe thousands in unpaid taxes).

For example:

I am writing because there is so much that I have wanted to tell you over the last month and so much that I have to apologize for. Every ounce of me wants to tell you how much I love you. But I know those words may not mean anything to you because of my lack of action over the years and the pain that I have caused you. It is because of your pain that I am writing and not having a conversation with you that might be disturbing for you.

I am deeply sorry for how often I neglected your wants and desires, for the many times you went to sleep crying because of things I said or did. I can only ask you to forgive me for the countless hours I spent at work or out, neglecting you and our family. I'm sorry for all the times I lived behind a computer screen instead of going for a walk, telling you how important you are to me, or taking 10 seconds to say thank you. You asked for so little, yet I didn't even manage to give you that.

You have done so much to take care of us all. You have sacrificed so many of your hopes and dreams to ensure that we could reach ours. And I never stopped to acknowledge this. I only criticized what you did and pointed out how it could be better. The profanity that could be used to describe me and my behavior through the years would not be pleasant, but it would be true.

I know that you have never felt good enough, but that couldn't be further from the truth. Although it was never my intention, the reality is that my actions communicated that to you repeatedly.

I am so sorry for all the neglect, for all the conflict, for all the unkindness you have suffered at my hands and mouth. I can only ask for your forgiveness and work each day to become the kind of person who would be worthy of your love. I have been in counseling for 8 weeks now and am seeing the things you told me all along. I have "homework" from my counselor, part of which is to attend Alcoholics Anonymous. I know I always denied having a problem, but my eyes are opening, and I go twice a week and have a sponsor. I know that I may never have the joy of receiving your love again. I don't deserve it. But you deserved this apology long ago. I don't expect a response from you. I just wanted to let you know and to ask you to please forgive me.

STAYING FOCUSED

You should also have some broken record phrases that you can use to keep *yourself* reframed. You will want to give up. Like the alcoholic who wants another drink, find your sponsors and make your plan. Write yourself notes, play relationship books in your car, podcast some seminars, find a song that makes you feel strong and listen to it every day. You know what works for you. Set a time, maybe right now, to think through this plan and write it out. Follow the 90% rule: ensure you are making plans that you are 90% likely to follow through with.

You are in for a difficult journey. **Learning to love, even when love is not returned, is a priceless skill.** Unconditional love is a treasure to learn, but a difficult task in which to persevere. It's easy to give up and cop out, saying, "There's nothing I can do." It's difficult to respond gently and lovingly, willing to give, yet expecting nothing, even in the face of the cold, hard, loveless winter. I do not envy your journey.

> *Learning to love, even when love is not returned, is a priceless skill.*

The ICU is not a fun place to live. You are not alone in wanting to take the nearest exit. You will feel like you can do it in one breath and want to give up in the next. The average journey is six to nine months, sometimes longer. This is about how long it takes in most crisis situations to "tip the scales." When I say "crisis situation," I'm not talking about a big fight or a disastrous office meeting. I'm talking about when your spouse wants a divorce, your teenager runs away, or you haven't spoken more than a few words to your boss in months. The six to nine months is not how long it takes for them to move back in or return home, though it might take that long. I'm talking about how long it takes before you're back on the road to "normal" again—for the scales to tip and for you to be able to share deep, meaningful conversation again. I have seen relationships in which one person has moved out, bought a house, and completely cut off communication, and yet one day slowly begins the process of rebuilding and reconnecting because of a spouse's unconditional love. But for those like yourself who are taking this journey for the first time, you have nothing but my word to go on.

We tend to have an easier time giving unconditional love to our kids. Say your son is twenty-four, and he's furious at you because his girlfriend doesn't think you like her. You were nice to her; she's just a sensitive, hormonal, twenty-year-old female. However, it's been two weeks and he hasn't called. He said he wanted nothing to do with you. Because we are better translators for our kids than we are for other people, you wisely realized those words were spoken in an emotional moment. What would you do? How would you respond to your son? And what if your love and kindness fell on deaf ears or were met with rejection? I know what most people would do: most people would plot, plan, and scheme how to keep loving their child, regardless of his response or lack thereof. And *you would not stop*. Whether it took weeks, months, or years, *you would not stop*. You might want to at times; it is only human. The roller coaster of emotion is human nature. Even with a child, you would sometimes want to give up. But you wouldn't, and almost every time, it would work. He would come back. You would reconnect again. This is how most stories end when we give unconditionally. I've seen it a hundred times.

It is a hard road, but your plan is clear. You have a singular goal: unconditional love. The great thing about this road is that it typically leads to all the places you want to end up: reconciliation, joy, happily ever after. It's not a road that will ever lead you to say, "I wish I hadn't done that." *Never.* It's a road that takes you to the richest lands imaginable.

HOW TO APPLY THIS TO YOUR LIFE:

The ICU is for people in critical condition. This is the time when unconditional love is mandatory. You must lead with compassion, understanding, and grace rather than with venom, tirades, and blaming. It's not always easy, but it's worth it. Let's figure this out. **What might this person be doing or saying because he is in protection mode?** For example, is she blaming you for all of the financial mishaps because she is in self-protection mode? Is he shutting you out because he truly cannot handle the situation right now? Perhaps he really does need some space to think and process. What signs of self-protection are you seeing in your relationship crisis?

Now that you realize they're in self-protection mode, you are also realizing that they are not equipped to handle your emotion in this delicate state. Remember the ICU room? How will you stay "positive, peaceful, and pleasant" and contribute positive, peaceful, and pleasant words and actions to this relationship?

What's the broken record phrase that is going to get your through this? (e.g. "I can do this. It's just a season. Spring is around the corner," "Positive, peaceful, patient," or the Serenity Prayer)

Write yourself a letter of encouragement right now, and include the following things: Tell yourself how you are going to get through this, step by step if necessary. Remind yourself of your coach and cheerleaders whom you can turn to when times get tough, but make sure to choose them carefully. Spell out your self-care strategy for the next several months. Write out your broken record phrase. Remind yourself of what you ultimately want, and tell yourself that you are willing to do what you need to do to get it. You'll want to write this in a separate place for better access.

Once you write your letter, make a copy—or two or three. **Where do you need to put these copies?** In your car? Office? Bedroom? Purse? Station your letters at places where you know you'll need the encouragement and the reminder that this is just one chapter in your book, the whole story has not been written yet, and what you do now impacts the ending!

15

Monoscope
Expanding our focus to be treasure hunters

> *"People are not disturbed by things, but by the views they take of them."*
> *Epictetus*

A coworker and I used to keep track of how many times the director said "uh, um." We would keep track of it during conversations and then email each other the total. Sometimes we would sit next to each other in meetings and keep tally marks of how many we counted. While we made it into a funny game, it initially drove us up the wall. We literally thought he was wasting hours of our lives with his uhs and his ums. This was just one of his many faults that we regularly discussed. He was a quiet, quirky man, and we often wondered how he'd ever gotten the job. We didn't have anything nice to say about him. That changed when one day, I found him in his office, head in his hands. I could see the quiet sobbing moving his shoulders. I wanted to step away, but something drew me in to ask what was wrong.

Through tear-filled eyes he shared with me the diagnosis of his wife's cancer. They had discovered it in a routine check-up; it was aggressive, and she only had a couple months left to live. He pointed to her picture on his desk and explained how they had been married for thirty-two years and that he just adored her. I only spent about fifteen minutes in his office, but those fifteen minutes changed my entire perspective. I refocused. In the midst of everyday work, I had easily noticed his quirks and shortcomings, so much so that they dominated my thoughts during our meetings. I had failed to see the kind, generous man I would eventually come to know. I hate to think of how many years might have gone by, seen only through my narrow focus, had I not walked in that day. I am embarrassed at how easy it was to overlook his strengths, which in time, I would discover were many.

At times we act like pirates on a pirate ship, carefully peering through our monoscope, on guard for the next time we'll be pillaged and plundered.

> "He left his shoes by the door again! Can't he even help out a little bit?!"
>
> "She didn't even thank me. She's so ungrateful for everything I've done!"

"These crazy kids! All they ever do is fight!"

"I've tried and tried, but all he does is find fault in my work. There's nothing I can do to please him!"

We tend to fixate on the negative moments in life, as we look through the narrow lens of our monoscope, and miss all the surrounding beauty in our relationships. We dwell on these moments, we let them stew in our minds, we discuss them with others, and, not surprisingly, they eventually become the predominant view of our relationship. At this point in time, we usually start making both ourselves and the other person quite miserable. Have you reached this point?

> *We tend to fixate on the negative moments in life, as we look through the narrow lens of our monoscope, and miss all the surrounding beauty in our relationships.*

Still, we continue looking through the monoscope, closing off our view of all the good things happening around us, until we begin to believe that there are no good things. Our default mode is to find fault, and when we look hard enough for something, we will always find it: "Ah, there it is again! He's so selfish!"

As a counselor, I hear this all the time. Married couples, coworkers, and roommates focus in on a few minor issues that have somehow snowballed into massive problems. We label a behavior or the absence of a behavior as extremely significant, and the more we focus on this behavior with our handy monoscope, the larger the perceived significance becomes until we view the entire relationship as completely problematic. But in reality, undone dishes, imperfect evaluations, and speeding tickets are just the normal stuff of life.

You see, as human beings, we tend to get caught up in trying very hard to understand *why*. Why did our spouse or coworker or kids do this or that? We usually assume the answer is negative: "Because he doesn't love me anymore" or "Because she's so controlling and selfish!" So asking why doesn't get us very far, and it doesn't solve our problems—in fact, if anything, it tends to magnify our problems.

It's like pi. Pi is the number 3.14. A man discovered this number, and for whatever reason, we can plug it into all kinds of equations in physics, algebra, and calculus, and it *just works*. We have no idea *why* it works, but it works, and it allows us to build planes, engineer bridges, and map trajectories. It's the same for our relationships: we don't have to figure everything out in order to find something that works. Perhaps it would do us good to throw our little monoscope overboard, stop focusing on the negative, and start thinking about how we can create change?

You may be thinking, "Yeah, but you have no idea how *crazy* he is!" And I would probably agree with you, but focusing on the craziness only makes us crazier still. Even when things are not our fault, even when the other person is clearly in the wrong, and even when they refuse to cooperate, we can still be the solution. We may have no power to change them, but we can change ourselves by adjusting our words, actions, and thoughts to reach a better outcome. **When we choose to respond differently, this will impact the other person and the relationship in a positive way. So despite popular belief, it only takes one to tango.**

> *...despite popular belief, it only takes one to tango.*

Now, finding a solution may be simple, but that doesn't mean it will be easy to implement. It's like losing weight: a fairly simple process, but definitely not easy. If it were easy, we would all be supermodels. In the same way, choosing to respond differently in our relationships is never easy; if it were, then we would have no relationship problems.

Let's say your son goes to school and little Bobby punches him in the face. He comes home upset and with a black eye. Whose fault is this? It's Bobby's fault, isn't it? It's true that Bobby chose to hit, and maybe Bobby really is a mean little kid who punches other children for absolutely no reason. Now, if you're a parent, you probably want to kill Bobby—or at least maim him a little bit. But since you cannot do this without getting arrested, allow me to advise you to come up with other solutions for the sake of your child. Bobby, believe it or not, is not your son's problem. *People are never the problem; the problem is the problem.* Getting punched in the face is your son's problem.

As much as we want to focus on the problem of Bobby, your child has no control over Bobby's mind, heart, or fists. But there are things your child has complete control over, and there are things your child can think, do, and say to improve the situation. For example, he can locate Bobby and avoid him, and if Bobby comes near him, he can go stand near the teacher. This is just one of many options available to your son to keep him from getting punched in the face, his real problem.

We all know that infamous phrase many parents use, to the annoyance of their children: **"When you point one finger at someone else, there are three fingers pointing back at you!" There are indeed three things we can do to improve our situation, one for each finger: we can change what we think, what we say, and what we do.** While the phrase seems silly, the person who said it first was exactly right, understanding that pointing fingers at others only leaves us

> *Remember, the other person is not your problem. The problem is the problem.*

frustrated and hurt, while focusing on our own thoughts, words, and actions will produce remarkable success. **Remember, the other person is not your problem. The problem is the problem.**

If we focus on trying to change Bobby, we will get *very* frustrated *very* quickly—not to mention our son might get more black eyes and hurt feelings in the process. But if we focus on solving the problem—what can I say, think, or do to keep from getting punched in the face?—we can have great success.

HOW TO APPLY THIS TO YOUR LIFE:

Ah, your own personal monoscope. It provides great tunnel vision, allowing you to focus in on those things that others keep doing wrong. Maybe your teenage daughter actually enjoys the chaos in her room because it sparks her creativity. Or perhaps you neglected to see that your wife did the bills that way because she thought she was being helpful. **Where are you using a monoscope?**

It's time to broaden your lens and take in a panoramic view. If you were to open up the lens of your relationship, **what could you see differently, in a positive light?**

People are never the problem; the problem is the problem. Ouch. That's going to change things a little the next time you're angry with your spouse for leaving the gas tank on empty or the next time your coworker drinks the soda you'd left chilling in the staff fridge. Who is one person you seem to have conflict with more often than you'd like?

Now that you know the person isn't really the problem, what is the actual problem? To identify the actual problem, try simply removing the person from the sentence and starting with "I." For example, instead of "My husband is lazy," the actual problem is "I want these dishes done." Be careful that you don't simply change it to "**I think** my husband is lazy" or "**I wish** my coworker would file these forms on time." Instead say, "I would like these forms filed on time." So, what's the real problem?

Okay, it's time to put on that thinking cap again. Now that you know the actual problem, what will you do to respond differently? Is it going to be a change in thought? For example, "She probably didn't mean to single me out." Perhaps it's what you will say? "Wow, you must have been thirsty." Maybe you'll simply fill that gas tank up yourself instead of starting an argument about it. Perhaps you'll get access and file the forms yourself, or you might learn that if you email your coworker first thing in the morning so that it's at the top of her inbox, it gets done more quickly. **What will you do to respond differently?**

16

Roadblocks
Removing the pain that plagues us

"The weak can never forgive. Forgiveness is the attribute of the strong."
Mahatma Ghandi

It was not her first affair. The tragic decisions that led to this pain were numerous. His heart was crushed. The pain hit so hard that it knocked the wind out of him. How could this happen, *again?* But years later, he explains:

"I still don't understand completely how the affairs could have seemed like the desirable thing. I really don't care anymore. I don't think a better understanding of why or how will make me trust easier or hurt any less. I even suspect that if I really understood why or how, it would be more painful.

Affairs in many ways feel devastating. The affairs in our marriage were no exception. I begged God for help. I didn't want to be divorced. I didn't want to be a weekend Dad. I didn't want to explain to our son why we were divorcing. I didn't want to damage the community where we were involved. One of the hardest parts was playing dumb sometimes, while I waited for her to come around. It seemed like the only way to move forward was to be willing to forgive my wife. Yet she seemed to work at being unlovable.

I'm a Christian, so I view forgiveness from the spiritual aspect. But I think the idea is the same for all. I prayed for God to help me to love her. I wanted us to stay married, but *I asked God to help me WANT to be with her, not just to do the right thing.* God gave me courage and, I believe, wisdom to know what to say or do and to be willing to act. In time, I gained love and compassion for her again.

One thing I had to realize was that, while I may not have ever slept with another woman, I have my fair share of failures that cause other people great pain. I had to come to realize that I "cheat" all of the time; I hurt and betray others. Yet God allows me to "run around on him" while he waits for me to come around. **Forgiveness is only hard when I think of myself as someone who doesn't need forgiven.** It is easy to feel like an innocent victim and forget my own 'criminal' activity. It is easy to minimize what I did wrong in light of the overwhelming pain I was experiencing at her hand.

> *Forgiveness is only hard when I think of myself as someone who doesn't need forgiven.*

A big part of my healing came when I realized my own need for forgiveness and it became the central part of 'our story.' How could I withhold forgiveness from someone while I continued to need forgiveness from others? When I saw myself for what I am, a sinful man in need of forgiveness, forgiving my wife became relatively easy.

It has been years now, yet I still hurt a little. I have never really trusted people anyway, and this didn't help. I have trouble believing that anyone really likes me, and this didn't help. I could list more fears and insecurities that the affairs tweaked, but I work to not give them voice. Instead, I choose to celebrate the truth that I know. I am forgiven and I am loved by God. *I choose to believe that I am loved by my wife.* None of this happened overnight. We both needed to give and receive forgiveness in order for our marriage to continue, and through time and continued refocusing, we are doing well."

By definition, no one ever *deserves* forgiveness. No one ever has a *right* to be forgiven—forgiveness is an act of mercy. So why choose to forgive someone who doesn't deserve it in the first place? That's a great question, and I'll tell you why forgiveness is good. Forgiveness is not really for the other person. Forgiveness is for you. In fact, forgiveness could very well be defined as a *selfish* thing to do. You see, **when you choose to forgive, you release *yourself* from the anger, the frustration, the hurt, and the disappointment you harbor**...and harbor...and harbor. Those people you need to forgive are living *rent free* in your head and heart, subjecting you to all

> *...when you choose to forgive, you release yourself from the anger, the frustration, the hurt, and the disappointment you harbor...*

sorts of misery. Evict them! Bitterness steals your happiness. Bitterness locks you up. Forgiveness sets you free.

You see, we evaluate all sorts of things as "wrong," and these evaluations drive us toward undesirable attitudes and actions in our relationships. Oh yes, I hear lots of things called "wrong" in my office: anything from leaving Coke cans around the house to not calling when you're running late. Sometimes it's subtle; "wrong" may be replaced with "*should* have"—but the message is still the same. "She should have picked up those cans!" means that by not picking up the cans, she did something wrong.

As far as I know, there's no commandment that says, "Thou shalt pick up your soda cans" or "Thou shalt always telephone thy neighbor when running late." The truth is that you *prefer* the person picked up the soda cans. This is your preference, not theirs, and it's certainly not a right or wrong issue. (And yes, I often use the Ten Commandments as a general moral guide by which to evaluate if something is truly wrong. Killing someone? Wrong. Not picking up the soda cans? Not wrong.) However, sometimes there *are* monumental wrongs and monumental hurts, and forgiveness is easier said than done. Gary Smalley, in his book, *The DNA of Relationships for Couples,* fleshes out some of the roadblocks to forgiveness that keep us from living that life of peace and happiness.[10] We'll summarize his five roadblocks here:

Roadblock #1: We feel like forgiveness lets the guilty party off the hook. We think that if they've not been punished or haven't admitted their mistake and apologized, they are getting off easy. But remember: forgiveness has nothing to do with that. Forgiveness lets *us* off the hook by allowing us to rid ourselves of the anger and frustration we've been feeling. Therefore, unless someone asks, we don't even have to tell them we've forgiven them. They may not even care or know how hurt we felt. Forgiveness is for us, so we can forgive and be free without needing to inform the other person.

Roadblock #2: Sometimes we believe forgiving means forgetting. You might say, "And just how am I supposed to forget that you cheated on me?!" Forgiveness does not mean you magically have the ability to forget. Forgiveness is a process, not a one-time event. When those painful memories are triggered, forgiveness breaks the cycle of pain as many times as it takes. It's not that we must stop thinking about it because usually we can't. It's that we must become committed to redirecting ourselves and thinking new thoughts. Because when we refuse to forgive, we live in a prison cell with those painful thoughts.

Roadblock #3: Sometimes our biggest roadblock is forgetting how often *we* need forgiveness. We forget about what we've done wrong or failed to do right. We daily say and do unkind things to each other. Sometimes we look at others and say, "I would never do that," which could very well be true. You would never do *that*. Your failings look different—everyone's failings look different—and there is likely a failing you have which another person would "never do." We are all in the same boat. Maybe he calls you names, but you cross your arms, shut him out and walk away thinking hateful thoughts.

You know that person who drives you up the wall more than anyone else? Guess what? *You're just like them.* **Universally, we all mess up; it just looks different.** Has there ever been a time when you lied? Ever said something rude or hurtful? How many times have you not admitted when you did something wrong? Is there any bitterness in your heart, any grudges you're holding on to? Have you ever retaliated against someone? Maybe you "forgot" to do something for them? Is there anything you deeply regret? You may have heard the prayer: "Lord, help me forgive people who sin differently than I do." We're all in the same boat.

Roadblock #4: Sometimes our biggest roadblock comes from festering anger or fear. *Walking the Forgiveness Path* offers enlightening information on how to deal with anger. I quote them extensively because they state it so well. It explains that when we indulge our anger, we retell the story over and over, which continues to give it energy and even escalates the anger. Here's the sad part we don't often notice: "…we consume our thoughts, emotions, and energy in ways that keep us from moving forward and growing; it is a case of 'drinking poison with the expectation that the other person will die.[11]'" We are hurting ourselves. The way out:

"It's choosing—asserting your will—to gracefully let go of the retelling of the 'I've been violated' story and replace it with one that is open to growth for yourself. When this shift in story occurs, it is accompanied by a shift in feelings. A movement away from anger, toward calmness.[12]"

"When not clouded with feelings of anger, our attention can turn to empathizing with the other person and their behavior. We might not fully understand the reasons that drove the other's behavior, but the reasons are there for sure. The past is over. It cannot be changed. Only the future can. We determine our future through the behaviors and thoughts we choose to have at this moment in response to the events that have already occurred.[13]"

Roadblock #5: Many people have difficulty forgiving when they feel like they don't know what they would do if the situation should reoccur. They feel threatened, unable to discern how to care for themselves in the future: "I can't forgive you because I really don't know how I would deal with this if it ever happened again. I can't forgive you because I'm still scared and upset. What if it happens again? What will I do?"

Play that out. What *if* it happens again? What *will* you do? How *will* you handle it? You will live, you will make it through. Play that out and work your way around this roadblock.

HOW TO APPLY THIS TO YOUR LIFE:

Forgiveness is really a gift to yourself. Who are you letting live rent free in your heart and head, allowing bitterness and anger to swell and take over?

Now imagine your life without all that bitterness and anger consuming you every time you hear their name or see their face. What would that be like? Write down five benefits for your life if you chose to live without the bitterness and anger.

What roadblocks to forgiveness are you having difficulty moving around right now?

How will you maneuver around that roadblock to embrace your new FREE life, a life of forgiveness, so that person is no longer taking up residence in your heart and mind? Be specific. **Write down your path to forgiveness. What are you going to do? When?**

Further reading:
Luskin, Frederic. *Forgive for Good.* New York: HarperCollins, 2002.
Smalley, Dr. Gary, and Ted Cunningham. *From Anger to Intimacy: How Forgiveness Can Transform Your Marriage.* Ventura: Regal, 2009.

17

The Golden Rule
Changing from referee to cheerleader

"Kindness is the language which the deaf can hear and the blind can see."
Mark Twain

All major religions have a Golden Rule. They may not call it that, but the principle to do unto others as you would have them do unto you is universal. And though the rule seems clear, I believe it's often misunderstood. I realized this when I was teaching graduate school. A psychologist named Tom worked across the hall from my office. One day, knowing Tom's expertise in parenting, I asked him for some guidance in dealing with my teenager.

We counselors often say that there are three types of people who walk into the office. There is the "customer," who wants to make things better. There is the "complainant," who wants to whine. And there is the "visitor," who really doesn't care to be there at all. On this day, in Tom's office, I was definitely a complainant. Tom only has so much time in his day and had heard just about enough of my whining. Keep in mind that Tom is a very tender and gentle man who typically talks at a level just above a whisper. However, he's also a 75-year-old, seasoned counselor. So as I was sitting there complaining away, Tom stood up behind his desk, slammed his hands on the desk, and raised his voice at me: "Are you just going to sit there and tell me how you've already tried everything, or are we going to figure this out?!" Then he sat back down and was perfectly calm Tom again. My response was a rather nonchalant "Okay."

This is *not* the way Tom himself would like to be talked to, but this is *exactly* the way to get my attention and help me refocus. He knows nothing else is going to get through my thick skull. However, if I did the same thing to some of you, you might be in tears. All of us prefer to be spoken to differently. So, really, we would never want to do unto others as we would have them do unto us in any kind of literal sense, or I would be yelling at a lot of you. The Golden Rule, at its heart, is about being a good gift-giver.

I'm guessing many of you have experienced bad gift-givers. I can't help but think of a Christmas shopping trip I took with some girlfriends. While browsing, my friend found this bizarre puzzle game and exclaimed, "Oh, I just love this thing! Don't you just love it? Who can I get this for? I know!

I'll get it for Jenny!" The problem is that Jenny doesn't care about puzzles, and she certainly doesn't need a puzzle. In fact, Jenny would probably dislike the puzzle. More importantly, there are a lot of things Jenny does need that my friend could get her. My friend has it backwards: she thinks being a good gift-giver is about getting the other person something she herself would love. **But if you want to give someone a really great gift, you have to think about what the other person would enjoy.**

If someone wanted to give me a really great gift, it would be mercy. **I don't know about you, but when I make mistakes and mess things up, I would love it if people would just cut me some slack.** If we really want to follow the Golden Rule and do unto others as we would have them do unto us, then we should be merciful. Who among us doesn't want mercy and forgiveness?

...when I make mistakes and mess things up, I would love it if people would just cut me some slack.

Sometimes in our relationships we become referees; we're out there looking for someone to break the rules and commit a foul. Then, once they make a mistake, we immediately pull out the yellow flag and administer the penalty: "Aha! He left his shoes by the door again! Foul!" or "Just as I thought! He didn't get the presentation done like he said he would!"

But wouldn't you love it if you could make mistakes and people wouldn't pull out those flags? Who wouldn't love that? I have a friend who is a wonderful mom, and one of her favorite phrases is: **"I have the opportunity to exercise mercy, and I'm going to give you mercy this time."** She acknowledges the wrongdoing, but she does not always have to carry out punishment; there are also occasions for mercy. Sometimes it's okay to just let things go. While it *is* our job as parents to teach our children right from wrong, it is *not* our job to do so with other adults. I imagine most people would love it if others could just let things go, quietly offering mercy, instead of blowing the whistle for every offense.

There are rare times when our perpetual behaviors become damaging to us and those around us, and in these situations, we do need a loving arm to take us aside, compassionately share concern, and help us find a solution. But this type of confrontation has the Golden Rule at heart; we confront because it's best for the other person, not so we can tell them how to change to make us happy or to tell them how much they hurt us. This kind of loving confrontation considers how the other person might best receive the information and how to move them toward what's best for them. This often means that instead of initiating a conversation, we use subtle statements to reframe or encourage positive alternatives, such as, "You're such a smart kid, I know you'll get that homework done. I'm so proud of you for working so hard in school."

My husband and I (Shannon) used to run a not-for-profit organization working with high-risk youth and families. This gave me the opportunity to work with teens in the juvenile detention center on a weekly basis. Following the Golden Rule, we offered both mercy *and* tender confrontation at times. The first thing I did when I met with a new kid in the detention center was to ask all about them. I was sent in to do an assessment, but I had a little more freedom than the staff members, so I took my time and got to know the kids. My first questions were never "What did you do to get in here?" or "Why are you involved with this stuff?" Rather, I asked them about the things they liked: "What's your favorite music, sport, subject at school, food, etc?"

By showing the kids that I cared, I earned their trust and some of the "confrontational" topics were actually received thoughtfully by the kids. So rather than sitting down on the cold metal bench at the cold metal table, surrounded by thick glass and cameras, and lecturing them about how they needed to change, I got to know them. We laughed a little, we smiled, they often cried, *and then I told them what I thought they did well. And I told them what they had going for them. And finally, together we talked about ways to change.* It didn't come across as confrontational, even though it was still the business of confronting the bad behaviors in order to make a plan for the new, more productive, more beneficial behaviors. **Your approach matters.** Mercy matters. **When we have a heart to truly, carefully follow the Golden Rule and mercifully deal with others' mistakes, we have the highest potential for success.** Whether with employees at work, our kids at home, or our spouse, exercising mercy will give us the greatest success.

> When we have a heart to truly, carefully follow the Golden Rule and mercifully deal with others' mistakes, we have the highest potential for success.

There are some problems in life that need solving and some occasions that do require a conversation. We have to figure out finances and who's picking up the kids and who's in charge of which aspect of the project. But again, when we work on solving these problems, we must think in terms of giving the best gifts, asking ourselves, "How can I say this in a way that would be well received?" Because **even more importantly than what we are saying is *how* we are saying it**. My (Nealy) husband of-ten quotes me in jest because, apparently, early in our marriage, I said this all the time: "Well, if you think that, you're stupid." How well do you think that phrase worked for me? All of our suggesting, criticizing, insulting—they aren't working very well for us, are they?

> *...even more importantly than what we are saying is how we are saying it.*

The wonderful thing about cheerleaders is that when the players mess up, *they don't say a word*. But when the players succeed or need encour-agement, they're out there cheering them on. Are you ready to give up your whistle and pick up your pom-poms? One of the best gifts we can give to other people—our spouse, our kids, our coworkers—is to put away our flags and whistles and surrender the job of referee. Instead of calling out their mistakes, we can cheer them on to success; it's much, much more effective.

HOW TO APPLY THIS TO YOUR LIFE:

What are some areas where you need to learn to be silent and put down the yellow flag?

What has that yellow flag cost you in each of those areas? For example, maybe you repeatedly nag your teenage daughter about her messy room, resulting in her slowly pulling away from you. Maybe when your coworker speaks up during meetings, you cut him off, and now he doesn't share his ideas anymore. Or maybe you are negative and upset when your spouse gets home from work, and now he comes home later and later.

Some potentially difficult conversations are necessary. There will need to be talks about finances, the children, and the future. But how you go about those conversation really does make a difference. What topic of conversa-tion with your spouse, child, or coworker usually creates frustration and hostility?

Perhaps it's your approach. **How can you change your approach to follow the Golden Rule**, so that next time you have that conversation, fur won't fly? List three changes that you will make to your approach.

In what areas could you pick up the pom-poms and cheer others on? How could you cheer on your spouse? Kids? Coworkers?

18

But Why?!
Letting go of "Why" and grabbing hold of "Now what?"

> *"Always focus on the front windshield and not the review mirror."*
> *Colin Powell*

I've had a lifelong love affair with ice cream. In my college years, I remember buying a gallon bucket of chocolate ice cream and polishing it off in days. But the best ice cream, in my opinion, is that which has been appropriately dressed. See, I don't like my ice cream naked. Being such a cold food, and with the mothering instinct that I have, I think it needs to dress warmly. Hence, I prefer it clothed in a nice, warm coat of hot fudge, wrapped in a scarf of caramel, and topped with a hat of whipped cream—one of those hats with the puff ball on top, that juicy red cherry. When this alluring temptation comes my way, I find it near impossible to resist a bowl…or two.

I see the second bowl of ice cream as good in one way and losing weight as good in another way. It comes down to the moment and which good we want more in that moment: the weight loss or the ice cream. Both have good and bad to them. Ice cream tastes good and is enjoyable, so of course I want to eat it. Losing weight is healthy, so of course I want to lose weight. Ice cream is fattening and caloric, so it has bad qualities. Losing weight means giving up a lot of enjoyment, so it has bad qualities too. In relationships, we often view others' choices as "bad" and can't understand why they would do that—but we also make choices that could be viewed as "bad." Again, it comes down to which good we want more in the moment: the weight loss or the ice cream. All choices have good and bad to them.

Perhaps your spouse stays late at work. You think that it's "good" for him to be at home, and you have "good" reasons for wanting him there, with which he may agree. But in that moment, work faced him, and it seemed "good" to get it done. Both are legitimate goods. He is not an evil person out to make you miserable by leaving you alone for another night! It's simply a value conflict. He probably wants and values both: He wants to get work done. He wants to be at home spending time with you. But work is in front of him, deadlines face him, and others are counting on him. (I know—so are you.)

So when you call, your "reasons" are not likely to motivate him to come home. Furthermore, if you are upset or critical, he is definitely not going to be motivated to come home to someone who is in a bad mood. Therefore, if you want to motivate him to come home, you have to give him a good incentive that draws him from his present good. More importantly, you have to keep in mind what *does* motivate him, not what *ought* to motivate him. We often fail because we try to tell others what they "ought" to do. If that were actually a successful way to motivate, none of us would make mistakes. We would all do what we "ought" to do. However, these things don't motivate us very often, so we must find out what actually works. We have to be creative in order to motivate our spouses, our kids, our employees, and our bosses.

I face this dilemma in my classroom. My students "should" want to learn how to be a good counselor; after all, they're in grad school for counseling. They "ought" to read their texts. But the fact is that, left to themselves, most would probably not read. However, if I give them an exam over their reading, this would motivate most to read. "Should" they read? Of course! My very first client was someone's suicidal 13-year-old daughter. Her life relied on the reading and studying I did. But most students don't read because they "should." However, many do read if they are graded on it. We have to do what works, so I test my students on their reading. Likewise, if the wife in the previous illustration really wants her husband to come home from work, she might mention that all she is wearing is a big red bow ready for him to unwrap. I'm guessing this might motivate him.

Another reason we don't understand others' behavior is because we don't share their values. I may value the taste of ice cream over the health benefits of weight loss. Some people simply cannot understand this because health is one of their highest values. It is not one of mine. I don't care to live a long life. As a matter of fact, I believe I'd rather die of a heart attack than to live for decades with a failing mind. I value quality of life over quantity, so I intentionally do not always choose a healthy lifestyle.

Our values differ from person to person. For instance, some of us are socially motivated while others are task focused (see the "Welcome to the Jungle" chapters). Thus, because I am not a socially motivated person, I see others chatting in the break room as "wrong." I don't value chatting. I could (and do) stay home all day, every day, alone, not seeing another person and joyfully accomplishing my tasks. I see someone stopping a task to socialize as "lacking follow-through." However, the socially motivated people might see me as impersonal. They think I am "wrong" because I won't "take time for others" and get too consumed in my tasks. It's this value difference that often has us looking at one another and wondering "Why would they do that?!"

Sometimes we don't understand one another because our values differ altogether. However, at times we don't understand others' behavior because our values differ in the moment. The husband, who stays late at work might actually value family time more, but he has a huge project at this particular moment and chooses to stay late. It's a short term value change; it only lasts for a season. This happens to all of us. A mother has a new baby, and she quits her job. For this season, her baby is a higher value. She may have been a hard charger before—and she may be again—but her values change for right now. Understanding people's reasoning for what they do is difficult because our values are always in flux and because different values motivate us in different moments. I might eat the second bowl of ice cream one time, and the next time I might not. We like to think that we are rational, logical creatures, and we are; it just depends on what rationalization and logic we buy into in the moment.

In reality, we can't always understand others, and we don't often understand ourselves. There are not always simple answers for why your spouse wanted a divorce, causing you great pain, or why the owner decided to sell the company, leaving hundreds without jobs. We can ask, but there is often no real answer to the question. There are a hundred answers, many of which they might not even be aware. This is difficult for us to handle. We naturally want answers.

It was not too long ago that Zack was taken by helicopter to the children's hospital in St Louis. The week prior he had been dizzy and experiencing headaches. Then he ran into a wall and almost passed out in shop class. By that Friday night, he was tingly and unable to think clearly or follow a conversation. He deteriorated so quickly that by the time they loaded him into the helicopter Saturday morning to take him to the children's hospital, he was no longer able to move his limbs, and paralysis was setting in. Not long after arriving at the hospital, he could no longer speak, and he finally stopped responding. Zack is like a son to me, so this was devastating.

They ran a series of tests but found nothing. The one test that they thought might indicate the cause, a spinal tap, could not be done successfully because he had so many muscles in his back. They kept coming up with nothing. By Sunday morning, with no real findings, they diagnosed it as stress. *Stress?!?* Yeah, right! Stress definitely causes paralysis in 48 hours. But no other explanation could be found; all the tests came back fine.

We felt hopeless and terrified. We feared the deterioration would continue and that he might die. Whatever it was, it was breaking him down—and quickly. With no real diagnosis, there seemed to be no hope of treatment. How could they know what to do, what medication to give, or what treatment he needed when they had no idea what caused this? Everything they tested for was coming back negative.

We didn't know anything. So many tests had been run, and so many pain killers had been given. Was he unresponsive because he was doped up on the medication that the hospital had given him or because of whatever was going on with him physically? We wanted answers! The entire weekend I lived in fear, stressed beyond belief, all for one reason—and not even because he was falling apart. I knew I could deal with his deterioration if I only had answers. If only I knew what it was. If only I knew what to expect. If only, if only, if only... But I did not get answers. So my mind raced to a thousand different places and fear engulfed me.

It didn't make any sense. And like my strong desire to find out what was going on with Zack, you may want a diagnosis in your relationships. It is normal. It is human. We long for answer so that we can make sense of things, so that we know what to treat and how to treat it, and so that we can brace ourselves for the prognosis; even if Zack had brain cancer, I just wanted to know. It's the same with you. You just want to know. Is this cancer in your marriage? Is your job beyond repair? If so, you will prepare for the inevitable. Or is this something that is treatable?

Sunday afternoon, Zack's symptoms began to subside. By Monday morning, he was walking again and even took a shower. He was released from the hospital. "Stress" was written all over his paperwork. It is all they could definitively give us. My own guess is that some infection or virus ran its course. His body had to fight hard—and almost lost—but eventually gained the upper hand. The conditions had to be just right for something like this to happen. He had been sick, his immune system weakened, and at just the wrong moment, the virus entered. Had it been a week earlier, it might have killed him because his immune system was so depleted. Had it been a week later, he would have been stronger and the virus wouldn't have had a chance. Your situation may be the same. The wrong conditions, the wrong moment, and something small occurred—something small that turned into something big. And like me, you got terrified and, engulfed with fear, you were angry at the absurd diagnosis, and you just wanted a clear answer.

But there was no answer to the question "Why?" So I needed to focus on "Now what?" If I focused on trying to get answers where there were none, I would be engulfed in frustration and fear. I needed to return my focus to the moment: what did I need to do now? I was not allowed to be at the hospital because I had the flu at the time, and he might have an immune deficiency disorder. There were quite a lot of things I could not do. But I needed to focus on what I could do. I could be a support for those who were there. I could call and check in on them, give them a place to vent, and help them focus on the positive. I could vent my frustrations to friends who were not emotionally involved, those who didn't really know Zack, rather than to my family, which would just make them more upset. I could make sure there was food at the house and gas in the car. I stopped focusing on the unanswered questions and the long list of things I could not do, and focused instead on being helpful and supportive, which was much more beneficial.

Sometimes we don't get answers. **Sometimes there are no answers to the "whys" that face us.** We just have to wake up tomorrow and keep doing the right things for the right reasons. This includes being understanding of others when we want to scream at them, "Why? Why are you doing this? Why is this happening?" **The real question is not, "Why?" It is, "Now what?"**

> *Sometimes there are no answers to the "whys" that face us. The real question is not, "Why?" It is, "Now what?"*

HOW TO APPLY THIS TO YOUR LIFE:

What is the "why" that keeps eating at you?

What is the "now what" that you need to focus on? What are the things you can do right now to improve the situation?

What will you do to get yourself back on track when your mind turns back to "But why!?"

We value things differently from those around us. Sometimes we have completely different value systems, and sometime it's just a momentary difference. What have you been telling your coworker, friend, kids, or spouse that they ought to be doing? Are you telling your friend she needs to start dating again? Are you telling your coworker to stop sucking up to the boss? Did you tell your spouse last night how they should put the dishes in the dishwasher? **What is it you're telling that person to do or stop doing that is really just a difference of values?**

19

Simple, Not Easy
Tipping the scales toward a positive, rewarding relationship

"We are all faced with a series of great opportunities brilliantly disguised as an impossible situation." Chuck Swindoll

It's January, and once again, I am starting the year with a new resolve to lose weight. I imagine that I am one of millions having this thought at this very moment. For whatever reason, the New Year fills us with renewed commitment and hope that *this* time, we *will* lose the weight and we *will* keep it off.

I'm not quite as delusional about it this year. Years of attempts, small successes, and too many failures to count have given me a more realistic perspective. Through a lot of trial and error, I have learned some important keys to a solid weight loss plan, which, for me, include keeping chocolate and ice cream as options in small quantities.

Weight loss is an interesting phenomenon that eludes most of us despite our best efforts. We sometimes develop elaborate plans, join support groups, watch videos, pay for gym memberships, and count calories or points. There are probably as many ways to lose weight as there are people who want to lose it.

In reality, weight loss is really quite simple. Aside from surgery, there is really only one way to lose weight: burn more calories than you consume. And there are typically only three ways to do that: decrease intake (eat fewer calories), increase output (exercise more), or both. Losing weight really isn't rocket science. It's simple...but not easy.

Despite how simple it really is, success seems limited to a few, and long term success to even fewer. Why is weight loss so elusive? Why do we have money problems? Why are we struggling in school? Why is our work performance poor? Why are our kids out of control? Why is our marriage suffering? The root of many problems in our lives, if we are ready to admit it, is our own lack of self-control. We have not yet figured out how to make ourselves do the simple things.

And yet, we all possess self-control...in certain areas of life. Some of us are not tempted by chocolate or ice cream, but if you put a bag of chips in front of us, we cave. Some of us have no problem smiling and nodding at our neighbor's absurd ideas, but when our employee shares his pipe dream, we cut him off at the knees. Some of us are capable of reasoning patiently with strangers but resort to shouting at our teenager. It's not that we don't possess any self-control; it's that in those potato chip moments, our emotions cloud our ability to reason and consider the long-term effects. We place our immediate desire for potato chips over avoiding a heart attack at age 45, like the one that killed our Dad. We place our desire to be right in the moment over having a great working relationship with our employee. We place our desire to complete a list of chores over fun time with our family. So, due to a lack of self-control, all of our best intentions and best laid plans, despite our great enthusiasm, have not yet met with success.

But success *is* possible. We *can* do it. But, like weight loss, we may fail a hundred times. We may learn a hundred ways to *not* succeed. But there are some things that *will* work, some things that *will* produce results. Through trial and error, I found 100-calorie packs to be a very successful weight loss strategy for me. I have greatly increased my weight loss success because somebody went to the trouble to put chips in small little baggies, so I don't eat the entire 16 ounces. Someone made mini chocolate bars at 50 calories each, so I don't consume 400 calories at once. Yes, the temptation to eat all of the mini chocolate bars exists, but I've had much more success grabbing one small chocolate bar, closing the pantry door, walking into the living room, and not allowing myself to open my 50-calorie friend until I am seated and tucked back into my snuggly blanket. This simple process has actually made it much, much easier for me to maintain my weight. But it took a while to figure this out. And, more importantly, it took me having a singular focus: I *can* do this.

It's so easy to rationalize and believe the lies we tell ourselves, lies which allow us to continue in our lack of self-control. Some of my common rationalizations for weight loss, you may also say about other issues. We all have our excuses, such as: "I'll start next week," "Just this once," "It's Friday," "I'm stressed, so I need this," and "My family needs me to be in a better mood." Sound crazy? We use the most absurd reasoning to allow ourselves to give in to the moment. And then, if we feel the slightest tinge of guilt, we call someone who will agree with us, someone who will say, "You're stressed" or "You deserve it" or "Just this once." It's quite an amazing process how we "support" each other, isn't it? It's so easy to forget that heart attack that killed our Dad at age 45 and put him right in the back of our minds. Or to quickly forget whatever we just committed to doing.

The bad news is that our brain actually hardwires these paths. The more we follow these thought patterns in life, the more engrained they become in our brain and the easier they are to travel the next time we encounter the same situation. We build a brain superhighway, allowing ourselves to continue failing to do what we know is wise and to avoid the guilt of doing so. This is why the simple things aren't easy.

But don't drive the car off the cliff just yet. Knowing this can be helpful. Knowing how our brain can trick us into believing these crazy and misleading ideas is one step closer to learning how to overcome it! If we can commit ourselves to doing what is wise, we can overcome our natural, human hardwiring and make new paths. Just like we built the first superhighway in our brain, we can carve out a new road that will, over time, become the new interstate we travel with ease to lead us exactly where we really want to go.

Most of us want to have great relationships, and this is a worthy path, a path we, the authors, have given our lives to help people build. We have traveled with many brave souls who have tried and tried again, overcoming years of failed relationships and careers to renew their resolve and find strategies that lead to their long term success. It doesn't come without trial and error. It doesn't come without a pile of mistakes along the way. But those who stay the path learn that relationships really are simple. These brave souls have reaped the rewards that come with rich, deep relationships. Their journeys have led to amazing marriages, close connections with their kids, and enriching business partnerships. We applaud you, because reading this book shows that you are one of these people. We hope you will find encouragement and a wealth of strategies for your journey within these pages.

Willard Harley shares a helpful analogy about how relationships are simple. He explains that **relationships are like bank accounts where we make deposits and withdrawals. The key is to increase the deposits and decrease the withdrawals.**[14] Compliments, quality time spent together, helping each other out with responsibilities, and simple acts of kindness make deposits in the heart. If we keep those deposits of love high and the withdrawals—fighting, annoying habits, forgetfulness, and mistakes—low, then our relationship remains strong. This is simple but not always easy. We know what to do but are not always good at getting it done.

> ...relationships are like bank accounts where we make deposits and withdrawals. The key is to increase the deposits and decrease the withdrawals.

However, like with weight loss, we can find the path that gives us success and keeps the scales tipped in our favor, where the deposits outweigh the withdrawals. We can have million-dollar relationships and reap the interest off our deposits with almost anyone, no matter how difficult someone might seem.

Sometimes the scales get tipped to near bankruptcy with all the withdrawals taking place. But if you will stick to it, you can tip them back again. However, keep in mind that there are often *years* of withdrawals that led to the pain and distance in your relationship and it might take years to recover. However, I have never had one client ever regret choosing what is wise over what is easy. I have never had one client who regretted making deposit after deposit, even when there was no return. Sometimes it takes a long time to pay off the debt and move into the positive again. You may not have even caused the debt. For some, the relationship is suffering because of an illness, a death, a crime, or past pain. I encourage you to stay the path and force yourself (because sometimes you do have to force yourself) to do what it takes to tip the scales and create a positive account again. Increase deposits and decrease withdrawals: it really is that simple. It's just not always easy to get yourself to do that. Don't allow yourself to believe that it isn't possible, because at one point or another, you will think this. You'll actually think this over and over in some cases.

If you could wave your magic wand and have a wonderful relationship with even the most challenging person in your life, I'm guessing you would want it. Some people, after years of trying and failing, may be thinking, "I'm really not sure that I would want it." That's your superhighway again, looking for the immediate relief, steering you away from the long term reward. Do not allow yourself to believe it's impossible! Just like losing weight, you *can* have that wonderful relationship. Up to this point, you just haven't found the right strategy. You haven't found what works for you or discovered how to force yourself to do the wise, simple things that you know will ultimately pay off in the long run. But *you can.*

We know that relational success is not a one-stop shop. This book is just one of many options that can help. So if you don't find a plan here that works for you, please don't give up, find it somewhere. Just like all those people out there who want to lose weight, but haven't yet, there are just as many people out there who want to have better relationships, but don't yet. You really can; you just haven't yet figured out how.

I don't know if you know the story of Lance Armstrong's struggle with cancer. While he may be a controversial personality, his struggle with this deadly disease was grueling and real. I listened to his story on audio book while I was driving. He overcame unbelievable odds. It was a trying and difficult journey with moments of hopelessness, but *he had such a strong resolve*. Doctors will tell you that patients who have resolve make it. Those who choose to live no matter what, almost always live. Those who are ambivalent have a lower recovery rate. Research has even proven this.[15] **Resolve is the key.** It is the key to surviving physical deterioration and the key to surviving relational deterioration. Take it from this doctor. I have seen Stage IV, end-of-the-line, terminal relationships that died, but I have also seen many that lived. The ones that lived were the ones where *one* person—and it only takes one—has the resolve to keep trying. For these people, the survival rate is unbelievable.

HOW TO APPLY THIS TO YOUR LIFE:

Recall that Dr. Brown said it takes just <u>one</u> person to breathe life back into a relationship. Also recall that she said our minds often get trained in that superhighway of thought. If you've trained yourself to think, "It's not worth it," "I'm better off without him," or "She doesn't care, so why should I?" then it's going to take some effort to create a new superhighway of thought. Let's start that new highway. **What more positive thoughts could you use to replace the negative ones for your relationship?**

You will not regret wise choices. It's always beneficial to have a huge surplus in the bank rather than a deficit, right? We all want +$1,000, not -$1,000. It's the same with relationships. What will you do this week to add deposits to your relationship? Maybe it's a word of encouragement or a simple acknowledgement of how hard he works all day. Maybe it's a "thank you" for folding the laundry. Or a "good job" for your coworker. Maybe you decide to run the errand for her. **What deposits will you make this week to invest in your relationship?**

Perhaps it may benefit you to actually keep a ledger, like a checkbook. **Write down all of the deposits and withdrawals you make.** It will give you a realistic look of what you are really doing in your relationship.

However, for the other person, it is best not to focus on the deposits that they aren't making or the withdrawals that they are. I'm sure you can think of things you want them to do that they are not doing, or things they do that you wish they did not do. But try to focus on all the deposits that they <u>are</u> making. This can put deposits in your heart and bring a smile to your face. Maybe your spouse doesn't help with the dishes but always mows the lawn and takes out the trash. Maybe your coworker tends to be late and flighty but has a streak of creativity that brings life to your presentations. **List deposits that others are making in your heart.**

20

Walls
Finding a way in

"Kind words can be short and easy to speak, but their echoes are truly endless." Mother Theresa

James and Neal were both engineers in a large firm filled with many fairly unenthusiastic employees. But James, on the other hand, was creative by nature and full of ideas. James' mind was constantly flowing from one idea to the next. Many of his "great ideas" were not very solid, but they often provoked thought and helped the team to think outside the box and eventually solve their problems. When he was first hired, James would regularly share his ideas with his coworker, Neal. Initially, Neal just listened politely. But it didn't take long for Neal to grow tired of James' many ideas, and he began to poke holes in them. Every fault that Neal brought up was true; there were shortcomings to a lot of James' ideas. But what Neal unintentionally did was take the wind out of James' sails. In time, James didn't share with Neal at all and began to share less and less in team meetings. A year later, Neal was promoted to supervisor over the engineering development team. It didn't take him long to figure out exactly who he needed on his team: James. His team, though full of smart engineers, lacked a lot of creativity, and he knew it. He remembered the "great ideas" James always generated, and more importantly, as a fledgling leader, Neal realized how James was a master at getting the creative juices flowing. But when he asked James to join his team, James declined. My guess is that James did not find Neal very trustworthy.

People tend to talk in extremes when they talk about "being trustworthy." We treat it as an all or nothing trait: either someone is trustworthy or they are not. We say things like, "I can always depend on Bob, but oh, not Sarah! Wow, did you hear that whopper she told at work last week?" We don't realize it, but we base our assessment on a particular weakness a person has or a few events that occurred. But the truth is that trustworthiness isn't all or nothing. We can all be trustworthy at times and untrustworthy at other times.

We each define trustworthiness a little differently; I like Dr. Gary Smalley's definition from his book *The DNA of Relationships*. He says:

"We are only trustworthy when we treat others in such a way that shows we recognize their incredible value and deep vulnerability. We must remember people are tender human beings, with tender hearts, and the words we say and the ways we respond to them will have an impact on these hearts. We may think we're tough, we may even act tough, but we are all vulnerable in some way.[16]"

I don't know about you, but if someone were to videotape parts of my life, I would be embarrassed to show them on the big screen because there have been times when I have not been trustworthy. Somewhere along the way, I failed to remember that there was a human being on the other side of the conversation. I can identify with Neal in that I have often allowed my weariness of someone's ramblings to show, forgetting the value that person has. Have you ever failed to be trustworthy with another person's heart? We're all guilty; we're all in the same boat here.

When we fail to be trustworthy, our behavior sometimes causes others to build walls to protect themselves. Whether or not we intend it, our actions can lead others to pull away or shut down. When James declined Neal's offer, he was building a wall around himself to protect himself from the pain he felt in his interactions with Neal. So what do you do when you think someone is building a wall? You need to respect the walls.

During a conflict, when the other person walks away from us or attempts to end the conversation, we sometimes go hunt them down. Just imagine someone outside the door of your house saying, "Hey! What's going on in there?!" You decide you don't want them in your house, so you lock the door. If they try to break down the door or start throwing things at the door, this certainly won't make you any more inclined to let them in. In fact, if anything, you might decide to lock it even tighter or barricade it with furniture. Attempting to tear down the walls won't make anyone feel safer and will only contribute to more wall building, locking up, barricading, and protecting. **We can't demand that others open up and let us in and talk to us.** We can't cry and make them feel guilty. We can't badger them or force them. We must simply respect that they are closed for business right now, that they are protecting themselves from something, and that **the way to get in is to make it as safe as possible for the other person.**

Imagine your spouse comes home with *that* look on their face. If, when you ask what happened at work, the response is, "I don't want to talk about it," instead of nagging them, you might instead say, "I can see you're upset, and I'm so sorry. I would love to hear about it later when you do feel like talking." Respect the emotion and respect the wall by giving them the space they need. Realize this may mean that they don't ever want to talk about it. That's okay too. Sometimes it takes a while before we can earn their trust by proving we are a safe and positive person with whom to talk.

However, some people are just not talkers. There are a number of ways to deal with emotion, but two main ones come to mind: we talk it out or we act it out. Those who talk it out may choose to discuss it with friends or family about problems, but others prefer to give their voice to journaling or prayer, never actually confiding in a person. Those who act it out tend to put their emotion into a task, such as building something, playing a sport, or going for a walk. You may have people in your life who don't say much, and despite the emotion reflected on their face, they may never choose to talk it out. As safe and trustworthy as you are, it may be that they are just not talkers. So how do you know? You could ask, but I'm guessing you might not get a very helpful answer. Instead, I recommend that you simply work to become a safe and trustworthy person, someone who responds with compassion and encouragement when others share with you. Regardless of whether the other person is a talker or not, this is a great approach to have in any relationship. Be a cheerleader, point out the good, and overlook the shortcomings, unless it's your job to do otherwise. But even if it is your job, such as the position of a boss writing an evaluation or a teacher grading a paper, you can still be both a coach and a cheerleader.

I once overheard a wife talking to her friend about how her husband didn't talk with her much. She gave her friend a recent example of when she had overheard him sharing with someone else. His boss had evidently come unglued when a project wasn't completed on time. The husband had been waiting for another team to finish their part before he could do his. The wife heard this because she was eavesdropping as he was talking on his cell phone to his brother outside on their deck.

The wife was bothered not only because he did not share this with her, but because he wouldn't even stay in the house while he was sharing it with his brother, almost as if he didn't want her to know at all. This was just one of many examples that she told her friend. She was terribly upset with him. "Why can't he just tell me things?!" she exclaimed. She wanted him to talk with her, wanted to share their life stories together. When they were dating, they had talked all the time, but now he hadn't said much in months. Day in and day out, he came home and went downstairs to his computer. She knew their marriage was weakening, and she explained to her friend how she had already "tried everything she knew." She kept asking him, sometimes even *begging* him to talk with her. She even followed him down to his computer room to try to carry on conversations. In her mind there was nothing else she could do.

Then her friend asked, "Let me get this straight. He was out on the deck talking to his brother about what happened with his boss, right? And he never told you about it?"

"No," the wife responded.

The friend continued, "So, if he had said, 'I had a rotten day. My boss chewed me out. The project was supposed to be done, but I can't finish my part until the other team finishes theirs. There's nothing I can do,' how would you have responded?"

"I probably would have said, 'Get over it,'" the wife replied honestly. At that moment, the wife started to realize reasons why her husband might not be talking with her.

You cannot force others to open up and talk to you, but you can change the way you relate to them so that they will want to start talking with you again. And when you do change—when you stop trying to tear down their walls and simply focus on becoming a trustworthy person for them—the other person will feel safer sharing more of their heart with you. It will take time. A few positive responses do not erase years of negative ones. But if we keep at it, brick by brick, the wall *will* fall.

> *You cannot force others to open up and talk to you, but you can change the way you relate to them so that they will want to start talking with you again.*

HOW TO APPLY THIS TO YOUR LIFE:

People put up emotional walls for many reasons. You may or may not have contributed to the walls barricading your spouse's, child's, or coworker's heart. Regardless of who helped build those walls, you need to show that you are safe and trustworthy by respecting that barricade. **List the people with whom you have not been trustworthy.**

List the things that you say or do that make others feel unsafe, as if they need to hide behind a wall.

Now what will you do to instead show that you are safe and trustworthy and that you respect their wall? Perhaps you will stop picking on your son when he tries to hide his emotions from you. Or maybe you will respect the fact that she said she doesn't want to talk about it right now and let her have some time alone. Why don't you ask him if there may be a time later that he would be willing to talk about it—and be okay with hearing "no."

21

Trigger Points
Humility is for the strong.

"Humility is not thinking less of yourself, it's thinking of yourself less." Rick Warren

I have a lot of cousins. They're good boys, but they're still boys. So I'm at a family reunion, sitting and chatting with my family, when the boys run up to me with that wild look in their eyes and introduce me to "Herbert." Herbert is a baby snake, and I am absolutely, positively...*thrilled.* I love snakes. I love all creatures. I am literally the type of person who rescues worms off my driveway when it rains.

So I scoop up Herbert and begin playing with him; he's wriggling around my hands, and I am having a *wonderful* moment. Then I see the boys' faces. They are so disappointed. Naturally, they thought, "If I bring a baby snake to my Auntie Nealy, she will scream and run in fear! Cool!" So they are experiencing this moment as one of deep disappointment. And then I realize my daughter is right next to me—and she is literally *immobilized* by fear. She could not even move away because she is absolutely petrified by the snake. **Same moment, *very* different experiences.** In the same moment, one person is thrilled, others disappointed, and still another terrified.

We all have things that just make our skin crawl. Cockroaches? Mice? Nails on a chalkboard? With my daughter, you cannot even *say* the word "snake" in our house, that is how much it bothers her. We all have these emotional triggers, often against our better judgment. Sure, it's easy to say, "What's the big deal? It's just a baby snake. He's more scared of you than you are of him!" While this is completely true, just remember that you're not even allowed to *say* the word "snake" to my daughter because it triggers such an intense reaction. There is no reasoning with emotion. There are things that cause us fear, sorrow, anger, and embarrassment, even when we try to fight it!

I see examples of this in my office all the time. One person is having a major emotional reaction, while the other is thinking, "No big deal." He might rant and rave, and for him it's nothing; you could yell right back at him, and he wouldn't care in the least. But for her, on a scale of 1 to 10, it's a 17. "But he's *yelling* at me!" she says, and he's thinking, "So what?" She doesn't like yelling. She is having one of these emotional trigger moments, and he has no idea he's making such a major withdrawal from her heart because to him, it's chump change. Same moment, very different experiences.

For me, nothing has ever triggered quite the same emotional reaction as when my daughter looked at me and coolly said, "...Whatever." On a scale of 1 to 10, this was a 93. Here are a few other common triggers I've found:

"You always" or "You never"

"You can't..."

"Fine!"

"Think what you want to think..."

"That's stupid..."

"Why?"

"..." (the silent treatment)

I believe the first thing we need to do is to evaluate our own triggers. If we are smart, we will try to overcome our overreactions to little things. If seeing my kids' shoes on the floor is a 9 for me, then I would be wise to reframe my thoughts and feelings and put "shoes on the floor" where it belongs, which is probably a 2 or a 3. If my coworkers constant interruptions are an 8 for me, I could remind myself that we all have bad habits to overcome and change my level 8 irritation to a level 2 or 3. Even though we all have automatic emotional reactions, we can reset these. After all, there are things we used to be afraid of that we no longer fear. So, step one would be to decrease my sensitivity, even to things that still really bother me.

Another big part of this is to realize that others are likely not pushing our buttons on purpose. To prepare us for frequent international travel, the military educates troops on cultural sensitivity issues. As a military chaplain, I am often given the task of educating, since cultural and religious sensitivities are closely tied. I remember informing the men that they were not allowed to show the bottom of their foot in a Muslim culture. This is highly offensive. Now, you might not think that this would be something you're inclined to do anyway, but many men in America sit with one foot on the floor and the other propped up on the other leg. So the bottom of your foot is visible to those around you, even pointing directly at the person sitting next to you. It was important for the men to remember this because this simple, common sitting position could end up strongly offending a local. We would constantly remind each other, since at the location where we were sent, we were able to leave the military base and interact with locals. Sometimes these reminders grew to be irritating because it was not a big deal in our culture, but it was important. If my troops were not careful, there could have been a huge emotional outburst over something we thought was inconsequential.

Like my troops, most people do not intend to be malicious. It is difficult to stop doing things that are part of your routine. We all have moments when our delivery is very poor and ends up hurting another person, but we don't typically intend to be cruel. Unfortunately, a conversation that starts out with a well-meaning suggestion can end with "I'm done! I can't ever talk to you about anything!" When conflict escalates and emotions are triggered, the temptation is to focus on the symptoms instead of the disease. We say, "Quit yelling at me!" only to hear, "Well, you stop judging me!" We not only focus on these symptoms, but we increase their significance too: "If you really loved me, you wouldn't yell at me!" But all the yelling, the stonewalling, and the belittling are just ways that we defend our-

> *The hurt is the disease, and their reactions are simply the outward symptoms showing us they are hurting.*

selves when we're hurting and scared. The hurt and the fear are the real issue. **The hurt is the disease, and their reactions are simply the outward symptoms showing us they are hurting**. Hurt, scared people do and say irrational things, so there is a danger of getting sucked into a spiral of conflict, instead of humbling ourselves to attend to the hurting person in front of us.

It is our job to be compassionate in these moments. We must be sensitive to the fact that things that might be no big deal to us could be very hurtful to others. While we know we cannot please everyone all the time, we can be kind and considerate enough to try. Don't think about how "wrong" they are, criticize whether they should or shouldn't feel that way, or explain how they need to "get over it." When others are emotionally reacting—perhaps overreacting in your eyes—keep in mind that fear and pain can be a strong driving force. **When someone is experiencing pain and acting out because of it, remember that we all have these triggers, and choose to respond**

> *When someone is experiencing pain and acting out because of it, remember that we all have these triggers, and choose to respond with compassion and humility.*

with compassion and humility. We all need this mercy at times. And my guess is that if you exercise mercy, your end result will be much better.

If you were raised how I was raised, then you were raised to be tough. I'm certain I heard the phrase, "Quit crying, you big baby!" from people in my family of all ages. Toughness is a value I know very well. Little did I know how tough humility is, both in the sense that humility is often a difficult choice to make, but also because **humble choices are only made by the strongest of people.**

In the book *Good to Great*, Jim Collins studies the most productive companies with the greatest success, those that outperform other companies at an unbelievable rate.[17] He discovered five factors apparent in the leadership of those companies, and one factor, above all, was present in all of the most successful leaders: humility. Humility will give you the most success you have ever experienced in life, in business, and in relationships.

In his book, Collins shares this story:

"Three young men hopped on a bus in Detroit in the 1930s and tried to pick a fight with the wrong man sitting at the back of the vehicle. They insulted him, he did not respond. They turned up the heat on the insults, he said nothing. Eventually, the stranger stood up. He was much bigger than they had estimated from a seated position. Much bigger. He reached into his pocket, handed them his business card, walked off the bus and went on his way. As the bus drove on, the young men gathered around the card to read the words, 'Joe Louis, Boxer.' They had just tried to pick a fight with a man who would be heavy weight boxing champion of the world in 1937 and 1949, the number one boxer of all time. They apparently said of Louis, he could knock out a horse with one punch. I struggle to think how he got that reputation, but the point is simple. Here is a man of immense power and skill, capable of defending his honor with a single devastating blow, yet he chooses to forgo his status and hold his power forever, in this case, for some very fortunate young men.[18]"

There was a small Polish woman who you may have heard of: Mother Teresa. Her cause has reached billions of people worldwide, and if you ever had the privilege to hear her speak, you would quickly recognize her most dominant characteristic: humility. The most humble people tend to be wildly successful in all areas of their life: work, marriage, parenting, etc.

After the conflict at my daughter's graduation (see the "Little Devil" chapter) during which I struggled between listening to the little angel or the little devil, I had a choice to make. After all was said and done, when we got in the truck to leave, I turned to her and said, "I'm sorry. I sure wish I could replay these last twenty minutes. I wouldn't have said it like that. I wouldn't have done it like that." And at that moment, I chose humility. She had been silent since the fight, but after hearing those words, we reconnected and enjoyed a wonderful ride to Georgia. I cannot tell you how thrilled I have been the few times I have succeeded in choosing humility. Most of the conflict I have in my life comes from my own pride, my desire to be right, or my need to win. I must learn to put the other person first. **Humility isn't giving in to the problem; humility is giving in to the person, because in that moment the person is hurting**. There is certainly an appropriate time to find a solution. But if the other person is drowning in their emotion, then trying to talk

> *Humility isn't giving in to the problem; humility is giving in to the person, because in that moment the person is hurting.*

about things in the midst of that emotion will probably not be productive. On the other hand, you must also recognize that you can humbly and lovingly hear out your spouse, yet still change bank accounts because of his gambling addiction or her financially detrimental shopping. You can humbly show compassion to your teenager, yet still give consequences. You can humbly discuss the missed deadline with your employee, yet rate them appropriately on their end-of-year review. Boundaries and consequences are often in the best interest of the other person. Humility the attitude by which you make these decisions.

General McChrystal, former Commander U.S. Forces Afghanistan, was once interviewed and asked how we were going to win the war. You know what his answer was? "Humility. Completely counter-intuitive." This is not the response you'd expect from a four-star general in the Army. Humility goes against everything in us that wants to react, so, for every one time we succeed in choosing it, we will no doubt mess it up ten times. But if we are wise, we will keep choosing humility.

HOW TO APPLY THIS TO YOUR LIFE:

What are some trigger points for you that cause you to react emotionally?

How can you reduce your sensitivity to each of your triggers? You might consider going for a walk, counting backwards, or playing your favorite song, but you will also want to choose a "script" —something you say to yourself to reduce your tension and sensitivity to your triggers. For example, "We all make mistakes" or "This is just a preference, it is not wrong" or "You can do this, it is no big deal."

When your spouse, kids, friends, or coworkers are emotional, **what are the typical symptoms that start to show up that would tell you they are hurting?**

How could you choose to respond differently? Think of a recent interaction that did not go well. **What would the humble choice have been in that scenario?**

Many times we have an opinion, but we don't hold it as strongly as the other person holds theirs—a scale of 1-10 can be a handy tool. So ask each other, "On a scale of 1-10, how much does this matter to you? How much does this bother you?" You may be surprised at what you learn. What behaviors or words do you use that trigger major withdrawals in the hearts of your loved ones? (If you don't know already, try using the scale of 1-10.) How might you work to change those behaviors or choose different words?

Who do you know who is a great example of humility? What is it about them that gives you the impression of humility?

22

Stop It
Figuring out what works

"The most important single ingredient in the formula of success is knowing how to get along with people." Theodore Roosevelt

Mornings before school could be a warzone in our household. A couple of years ago, I (Shannon) noticed that I was doing something to fuel the fire. I am *not* the quintessential morning person, and in the early morning hours before school, I would notice and pick out all of the things my kiddos were doing "wrong." And not only that, but I would badger them about it. Ugh. No Mother of the Year Award here. A one-way conversation would go something like this: "Cassidy, how many years have you been getting ready for school? Yes, six years. Six years. And for how many years have you had to brush your teeth before we leave for school? Yes, six years. So why, after six years, do I still have to remind you to brush your teeth, especially when it's already past time to leave?" How many times did I say "six years" as a not-so-subtle reminder in just five minutes? I would quietly scold myself for badgering my kiddos once we were in the dead silent car. Then I would apologize while somehow making my badgering their fault.

Have you ever been there? Please say yes, so I know I'm not the only one! I simply needed to "Stop it!" I would never have done that in public. I do have self-control. I know my badgering was not in any way helpful to my daughter. Do you know what I did? One day while my kids were at school, I made a sign for myself, for my eyes only. It was a picture of a badger in a circle with a red line through it to remind myself to stop badgering my kids. And you know what? It took me some time, but I eventually stopped my badgering. To this day, when before-school issues arise, I remember the badger picture and "Stop it!"

You've already practiced "Stop it," and you're probably already quite skilled, at least when the public eye is on you. Sure, you may attack your children or your spouse or your coworker in private, but in public you manage to say things quite differently. So you do, in fact, have the ability to control yourself. When you feel your buttons being pushed, you can choose to react differently.

When I (Nealy) reach a certain point, my automatic response has become, "I am not in a good place right now; we need to talk about this tomorrow." I have found that when my buttons are pushed, this method of postponing the conversation is enormously successful for me. I used to be under the false assumption that I could talk about the problem the same day, but this rarely worked. I need a full 24 hours. Some people may only need thirty minutes. The point is that you must become a connoisseur of what works for you in your relationships. Here are some other ideas that may work for you:

Walk away. Time-outs are very effective for many people because they allow us to calm down and regroup. For the sake of the other person, you may need to say, "I just need a moment to calm down." If someone walks away from me, I will often follow them; others may feel hurt if you walk away. A brief heads-up of "I just need a moment" can help communicate your intent to calm down without the other person feeling hurt or feeling the need to follow you. It can also be beneficial to agree ahead of time on a phrase or signal to use in the midst of conflict. For example, agree in advance that when one person says, "Yellow flag," both people take a time out.

Be creative and unconventional. I used to teach school in some pretty rough areas of Chicago. When you yell at your classroom, you get nothing, but everyone magically quiets down when you start whispering. It would certainly be more difficult, and more humorous, to argue when you've committed to whispering. I know couples who use unconventional methods such as holding hands, putting on the other person's shoes, or even stripping down to their birthday suits, to keep tempers at bay during conflict. I've heard of coworkers who pass "the talking frog" to give each person a chance to speak. Creativity and humor are your friends, so do whatever works best.

Learn to agree to disagree. Disagreeing can be an effective skill to learn because in many cases, our default mode is to win the argument. Learning to say, "It's okay that they think x, even if I think y" will benefit everyone. Even if x is something we believe to be inaccurate, if x isn't going to kill them, it's okay for them to think it. Sometimes it takes pinching yourself or biting your tongue to remind yourself that it's okay to agree to disagree. The benefit of realizing that x is okay, even if it's not y, is that you are validating the other person's opinion and creating peace in the relationship. Arguments are often ongoing, hurtful, and depleting for the simple reason that we continue to try to get the other person to agree with us. Many conflicts would end if we could simply allow another person to think, say, or do things differently than ourselves, even if we believe them to be wrong. Even if we do think someone's perspective is damaging, conflict is not usually the solution; our words have not worked thus far and are unlikely to magically work the tenth time we try to explain to the other person how wrong they are.

Mind your own business. Whose life do I have the right to speak into? My children, my employees (those who I pay to work for me), and anyone who asks for my input, which then allows me into the area about which they are asking. All other people and situations are really none of my business. By that I mean that we have this grand idea that we should let people know whenever they're doing something that bothers or hurts or inconveniences us in the slightest. Or, we find ourselves wanting to "help" others by giving them advice. Most of the time, we just need to keep our mouths shut and mind our own business. For instance, Joe's employee, Mike, was having some problems at work. Mike was continually turning in his reports after the deadline. Not only did this display poor performance, but his tardiness impacted other departments' schedules. It would be appropriate for Joe to speak to Mike about this particular work issue. However, while Joe is talking to his employee, Mike brings up briefly how frustrated he is with his wife for going on a shopping spree over the weekend. Joe's employee's wife's shopping spree is simply not his business. So whether Joe thinks Mike should sit down and talk to his wife, take away her credit cards, or retaliate by going on his own shopping spree (and by the way, I hope you realize that not all of these are good options!), it's simply not his business, and he should not get involved. Now, this doesn't mean that we can't sometimes offer people helpful information, such as sharing that the appliance store is having a sale when your friend mentions needing a new dishwasher. But overall, we need to allow others to handle their own lives and offer opinions only when asked.

Harness the power of the replay. Our brain tends to take the path of least resistance, choosing paths that have already been traveled over and over again. You may find that you are unable to "stop it" until you rehearse it over and over again, creating alternative neural pathways for your brain to travel. Our brain forges superhighways for information that has been traveled over and over. So if we have a superhighway in place for a bad habit, any new good habit will take a while to form. At first, the neural pathways will be small and narrow. The more we rehearse the new good habit, the more deeply we forge the pathway. In time, the new good habit becomes our default mode, a new superhighway of good, productive behavior. Replaying productive thoughts is one of the most powerful paths to change.

This is also why our friends, family, and coworkers promise to "do better" next time but often fail. Their bad habits have also become superhighways, and changing them takes time. What is the behavior or thought process you want to change? Play the whole scenario out, right to the end, but replace your old behavior with the new, more productive behavior. You don't have to be in the situation to do this; your imagination will work just as well to embed this new circuitry. Replay and rehearse as much as possible: rehearse while you're driving to work, rehearse while you're cooking dinner, rehearse while you're brushing your teeth in the morning. Your brain has now stored a new and wiser pathway, whereas before, it traveled the superhighway to negative and harmful behaviors. So when you're running late, but he wants to leave, you no longer go down the road of conflict. You're ready with a new, calm response: "I'm sorry I'm not on time, but please go ahead without me—I'll be there soon." Perhaps this new response will trigger anger in him, but you can even imagine yourself smiling as he rants and raves. You're not responding and you're not fighting; you're choosing a new way of being. You can stop your automatic and emotional brain response from hijacking your rational thought.

Give it time. There was a time in my life when I did not allow myself to readdress a conflict for an entire month. Most of the time, by the end of the month, I no longer felt the need to address it. What had seemed like an issue at the time really wasn't anymore. I was simply upset and "addressing it" was a way to deal with my anxiety. When I gave it time, I found that my anxiety went away without ever having to address it. I find most "issues" to be this way. There are very few that actually require a constructive win-win solution. Many issues are just my own momentary frustration, and, if given time, there is no need to bring it up again.

Whichever of the above methods you choose to "stop it," we need to be doing the right things for the right reasons in the right ways. You may want to read the chapter on the Golden Rule to help you go about instituting change for the better, in ways that make the change as easy as possible for all involved. Sometimes change, even positive change, is not readily received by the other person. We should expect there to be a time of transition when others might not like the changes or might be uncooperative.

> *...we need to be doing the right things for the right reasons in the right ways.*

You may need to be prepared for the "screaming baby phenomenon." There comes a time in many parents' lives when they allow their baby to learn the skill of falling asleep on their own. Needless to say, the baby usually starts screaming, and if the parents do not immediately pacify the baby, what does he do next? He screams louder and louder. But eventually the baby gives up, accepts the new way of doing things, and learns to fall asleep on his own. Likewise, the first few times you try some of these tactics, you may expect the other person's emotions to escalate; maybe they'll yell, throw things, criticize, or give you the silent treatment. But if you stay your course, this escalation will subside, and the other person, like the crying baby, will become accustomed to the new wise and loving way of relating. Be prepared to weather the times when the other person will continue escalating until all their reactionary responses are exhausted. Also, be sensitive and humble in how you choose to make these changes. The goal is to do both what is wise *and* what is loving. Think again of the crying baby, and the mobile at the top of his crib. If you move one piece of that mobile, all the other pieces reposition around it. **If you begin behaving differently, you can change the entire system to something positive. It only takes one to tango.**

HOW TO APPLY THIS TO YOUR LIFE:

Think of an area of your life in which you need to tell yourself to "Stop it!" Perhaps it's with your kids before school. Or maybe it's what you say to your coworkers about your boss behind his back. **What do you need to stop doing?**

We've listed some possible methods to help you "Stop It" in this chapter. **Which of these methods, or what other method might you use, that would work best for you?**

How and when will you start to implement this new method? How will you make this method work for you? Write out a detailed plan.

23

As Is
Accepting the shortcomings of others

"*Everything has beauty but not everyone sees it.*" Confucius

My guess is that some of you out there like shopping, though what I'm about to say is still important even if you don't. Among those who are shoppers, I'm guessing that there are a few professional shoppers: the ones with an eye for spotting clearance racks, perhaps even brave enough to venture into the "as is" section. Not everyone is this brave. In America, we expect that whatever we buy will come in good working order. For the most part, if a store finds defective merchandise, they return to sender. But there are some stores that place these items out for sale, clearly marking them "as is," so there is no expectation that they're in perfect condition.

Being the professional cheapskate that I am, I was shopping at an "as is" rack myself one day. I even have a checklist already in mind for shopping on such a rack. So when I picked up a white blouse, I checked it over carefully. Were there any tears? Stains? Broken zippers? Unraveling seams? I even went the extra mile to carry it into natural light because those yellow stains can sometimes be hidden by fluorescent light. The blouse passed every test. So I slipped it on, checked it out in the mirror, and concluded that I had found a rare treasure. I double-checked the tag to make sure that it was indeed "as is" in case it had been placed on the wrong rack. Sure enough, today was my lucky day, and I made my way to the checkout with a new white blouse for $5.86.

One day before work, I was almost ready to go. I had my hair fixed and make-up on, and with a few minutes to spare, I donned my new white shirt. Much to my dismay, this treasure I'd found turned out to betray me. As I went to button it, I found all the button holes sewn closed. I paid my way through graduate school by sewing, so I knew enough to check if they had simply failed to slit them open. No such luck: these babies were crossed over and sewn closed.

Needless to say, I was not a happy camper. That's how we feel when we encounter an "as is" item, isn't it? I thought I'd found a good deal. I thought this shirt was going to serve me well. Then, lo and behold, I've been ripped off, scally-waggled, betrayed. But the fact remains that the advertising had not been false: the sign read "as is."

I need to expect that everyone I encounter is "as is." Just like the clothing on the racks, we each have our own version of "as is." Some of us are quick to speak without thinking, and we wound hearts with our hurtful words. Others of us sit and stonewall in our anger, and we wound hearts with our silence. Some of us are given to work so much that we forget the people who mean the most to us. Others may give full attention to those people but fail to ensure that responsibilities are complete. I might have defective button holes, while you have a broken zipper.

We all have those moments though, the moments when we forget where we're shopping and somehow expect people to be perfect. And then we encounter their less-than-perfect side and feel ripped off. We forget about the fact that we're "as is" too. I might encounter someone with a broken zipper and forget about my button holes. I might even think to myself, "I would never do that." And I'd be right, because that's not my weakness. But we're all in the same boat; we all have weaknesses. I might not do that, but I would do…well, the list is too long, really.

Let's look at this concept another way, in terms of virtues. If we think of virtues like patience, kindness, self-control, and perseverance, we can quickly see how we're all in the same boat. I might be upset by your road rage because I don't struggle with road rage, but my impatience shows up in other ways, like when I yell at my kids. We are all impatient. When we look at the specific action, the road rage, instead of considering the virtue of patience where we all fail, it's easy to think, "I would never do that." But the fact is that we all fail to live virtuously; our failures just look different. Likewise, I may think your spending is out of control and insist that I would never do that. But I have other issues with self-control—we all do. There is not one of us who has mastered a single virtue; we all fail at every virtue at certain times. I might be better at some virtues than others, but there is always room for growth. Therefore, I need to remember that you and I are in the same boat. We each have our own shortcomings in every virtue; they just look different.

As a counselor, I've learned that pain comes in all shapes and sizes. I'm humbly reminded that I cause hurt, just like others have hurt me. I used to be quite a hot head. Age and maturity have grown that out of me somewhat, but I typically speak long before thought enters. Decades later, I'm still working on my "broken filter," and I may struggle with it for decades to come. Thank goodness the people in my life haven't given up on me! Author Lysa

TerKeurst says, "Friends are a package deal. And sadly, not all friendships will stand the test of time. Some friendships are for a season. But other times, we have to be willing to deal with the messy stuff to fight for our friendships.[20]" Everyone you meet is an "as-is package deal."

Let's say Bob hates the fact that his wife, Mary, smokes. He is literally afraid for her life. His father died of lung cancer a few years earlier, and Bob watched him slowly waste away. Bob repeatedly asks Mary to stop smoking. In fact, he usually begs her to quit at least once a week. He's hidden her cigarettes and even thrown them away. He's signed her up for classes to help her quit, bought her nicotine gum, and made her an appointment with a hypnotherapist, though she did not go. Bob is a very unhappy man, and his repeated nagging and degrading remarks about this "nasty habit" are taking quite a heavy toll on their relationship. His lack of acceptance is costing him a lot in his own frustration. It is costing them both a lot in their relationship. **Lack of acceptance costs us far more than we really want to pay.**

Lack of acceptance costs us far more than we really want to pay.

In our relationships, we often look to the other person to make us happy. Bob is making Mary entirely responsible for keeping him happy: "If she would only quit smoking, things would be fine! How can she do this to me!?" Though you might not be in Bob's exact shoes, I'm sure you could fill in the blank, be it with your spouse, your kids, or your coworkers: "If only they would _____, then things would be fine!" We forget that everyone in our lives is an "as-is package deal." But let's say Bob decides to stop making Mary responsible for his happiness. Let's say he decides to accept her "as is" and starts taking responsibility for his own happiness. After all, if you want it, you're responsible for making it happen. What might that look like instead?

Bob still wants Mary to quit smoking, but he decides to stop battling with her, allow her the freedom to make her own decisions, and accept her "as is." Bob joins a grief support group at his church to work through his feelings about his Dad. Whenever Mary smokes, instead of nagging her and starting a fight, Bob simply takes a walk or visits with his neighbors. Since Mary smokes quite a bit, Bob becomes great friends with his neighbors over the years. Though Mary continues to smoke, Bob and Mary no longer have nasty arguments. In fact, they start spending more time together, and because Mary doesn't want Bob to leave during these quality times, she refrains from smoking in his presence.

We don't have to agree with what they do or condone their decisions to accept them as they are. Furthermore, lack of acceptance is quite costly and can keep us from having a good relationship. Bob has learned how to *honor* Mary. When we honor people at retirement parties or funeral services, we do so by overlooking their flaws and focusing on their strengths. There is a certain way that we talk about the people we are honoring them. They don't even have to be the most honorable people, but we can still treat them in honorable ways. Unfortunately, we often act very dishonorably toward the people in our lives, insulting each other in public, pointing out what the other person does wrong, or shaking our heads condescendingly. Author J. Grant Howard, Jr. said about marriage, "We have the picture of a perfect partner, but we marry an imperfect person. Then we have two options: tear up the picture and accept the person, or tear up the person and accept the picture.[21]" **The choice is yours—choose to accept the people in your life "as is."**

> We don't have to agree with what they do or condone their decisions to accept them as they are.

HOW TO APPLY THIS TO YOUR LIFE:

Who is that person or people in your life who you need to accept "as is"? Is it that co-worker who is loud and obnoxious, your brother who parties too much, or your teenage daughter who has fallen in love with black eyeliner, weird music, and odd friends? Who are your "as is" people?

What specifically have you been trying to change about these people? What is it that they do that drives you crazy? Is it his smoking habit? Is it her messiness? Perhaps he's lacking the work ethic that you think he should have. What are you trying to change about them?

What is a lack of acceptance costing you? For instance, how often are you frustrated by this person? It's costing you happiness. How many fights have you had when you could have been enjoying each other? It's costing your relationship.

Now that you have pinpointed what you're trying to change, let's get real here. You can't make someone change. It's just a fact. You can plead, beg, and cry over it, but they have to make the change for themselves. And that only happens when and if they want to do it. So instead of focusing on them, let's focus on you. What can you do to make yourself happy? Instead of letting their lack of change bring you down, change yourself, like Bob did with Mary's smoking. What can you do to make yourself happy and stop focusing on changing the person you mentioned above?

Now, the even better question is: **when and how are you going to make the change in <u>you</u> happen?**

24

Self-care
Making sure you're at your best

"Take care of your body. It's the only place you have to live."Jim Rohn

For Cat Li Stevenson, life was good. She worked hard. She played hard. She even managed to maintain regular visits to the fitness center, despite her busy life, and she finally ran that half marathon. Everything seemed to be in place, and it only got better when she found out she was pregnant. She shares her story:

"While traveling overseas, I became pregnant and felt so much joy. My heart grew ten times bigger. It was that same bliss and expansion I experienced with my baby sister. After seven weeks, we learned that there was no heartbeat, and we'd lose the little bean to the universe. I remember feeling overwhelmed by grief for a few days and then bounced back literally as quickly as I could. I was back at the gym, running full speed a few short days after my surgery.

A few days later, I became very busy trying to lease out our current home and move into the new one. I remember my mother-in-law expressing sincere concern for me. She said, 'Cat, I don't mean to be hard on you, but you're doing too much.' I remember becoming very irritated and defensive. I responded, 'Don't worry about me. I know it seems like I'm always doing things, but I really do take good care of myself.'

After all, I worked out six days a week. I ate healthy meals. I drank 64 ounces of water daily. I had girl lunches. I had weekly date nights. I scheduled massages when I was stressed. And, on most nights I even slept a minimum of six hours. I took good care of myself—on the outside.

On the inside, I buried vulnerability. I played the resilience card. I sought out quick-fixes. And I convinced myself I was okay. I wasn't taking care of myself emotionally at all. Unconsciously, I placed

'I'll deal with it later' labels on several situations when they'd trickled into my life unplanned. Somewhere along the overachieving path of seeking perfection and always looking into the future, I lost myself when these labels accumulated. I managed to forget how to take care of my inner world.

After neglecting what was really going on in my life, I ended up in a curled-up ball in our bedroom corner, head buried in my knees, feeling a heavy amount of pain all at once...I made a decision to wake up each day, wholly, by connecting to who I am—to nurture myself from the inside out, to be with life instead of delay it—and, in turn, my days started to become more inviting again.[22]"

We are all driving through the journey of life together, but some of us are rolling on flat tires. We're either exhausted, stressed out, stretched too thin, and hanging on by a thread, or we're constantly irritable and mad at the world. This is what happens when we don't take care of ourselves, when we're spent and empty, like a flat tire. I don't know about you, but the ride gets pretty bumpy when I have a flat tire, and I can't get to where I'm going very well. When one tire is flat, the whole car rides poorly. Likewise, when we don't take care of ourselves, our relationships don't go very well either.

When you're on an airplane, what does the flight attendant always say? "Put your oxygen mask on first, then help those around you." You are no good to anyone when you can't even breathe. While there are certainly times in your relationships when you will go the extra mile, when you will sacrifice and expend extra energy for the other person, this should never be the norm. Why? Because there are big consequences when you continue to drive a car on a flat tire instead of pulling over. **You can do great damage to your relationships when you're continually running on empty**.

> *You can do great damage to your relationships when you're continually running on empty.*

Sometimes you can circumvent flat tires altogether with a little routine tire pressure check. I check my self-care every month, in four parts. I have a reminder to "Assess Self-care" that pops up on my calendar, and I sit down and check every tire. How am I doing physically, emotionally, mentally, and spiritually? Not everyone sees themselves as composed of these four parts, but whether you see yourself as one part or seventeen, caring for those parts will help keep you running smoothly.

Self-care is different for everybody. Self-care is anything that fills you up, refreshes, or restores you. For some people, reading quietly in the library is wonderful self-care. For others, this is like a death sentence because they get their energy from being around people. You will have to choose the self-care that energizes you most. What is going to fill you up so that you have plenty to give in your relationships?

Remember, we want to think about long term benefits; sometimes something that feels good short term can actually cause more harm than good in the long run, such as drugs, both illegal and prescription. Sometimes your brilliant self-care ideas will fail, and you'll have to brainstorm and rework your plan. This is why I reassess mine monthly, because some ideas just don't pan out. Maybe you love to swim, and you'd like to exercise every other day, but because the swimming pool is always closed when you're free, it's just not an option. So maybe you decide to put a treadmill in your office, walk at the park during your lunch break, or join an exercise class. Be creative and make sure your plan is simple and easy to ensure you'll follow it. Your self-care is too important to neglect.

Sometimes you will have to go outside your comfort zone to obtain the self-care you need most. Self-care isn't always the easiest thing to do for ourselves. If you're a workaholic, it won't necessarily be comfortable to get the rest and restoration you really need. Maybe you'd prefer to drink eight cups of coffee a day just so that you can just keep working and working instead of sleeping, but how well is that going to turn out in the long run? Or maybe you're one of those people who lives by their schedule and their to-do list, causing you to miss out on all those spontaneous self-care opportunities because you just can't adapt. If you've got cleaning planned for the day, that doesn't mean you have to clean. Sometimes you can say, "I'll do it later. It's gorgeous out, and I'm taking the kids to the beach today." And maybe while you're at the beach with the kids, it takes a little while before you can relax and unwind and stop thinking about the messy house—but it's hard to keep worrying about those undone dishes when you're helping your kids build a sand castle.

For all of us, self-care can be a crucial part of life. And there are some seasons where we need it more than ever. I ran across an old letter from a client that she had written for one of our sessions. She had her own demons to fight, sometimes leading to suicide attempts, but she kept managing to make it one more day. I asked her how she made it. She gave the usual "I don't know." So I asked for her help to think about what works for her because others needed her help. I asked if she would she write a letter to another client to tell them how she made it because, somehow, she *was* making it despite the demons she faced. It was her homework for the next time she came to session, and this is what she brought me. She said I could share it as long as I didn't mention her name.

"There're not many days that go by that I don't have to lie to myself to get out of bed. I have developed an interesting system. Psychologists would call it a 'coping skill.' I call it stupid. I lie to myself. I tell myself that if I get up, I won't make myself do anything but get a cup of coffee. A cup of coffee—that's it. Then if I want, I can go back to bed. Just going to get coffee…

This is a game I play each morning, and then again a few minutes after that and a few minutes after that. Some days more than others. First it's 'just coffee,' then it's 'just an email' or 'just a phone call' or 'just getting groceries.' Simple, doable, low expectations—some desirable, some I have to reward myself with, 'If you *just* do x, then you can do y.'

One would think that, being aware of this game, it would somehow not work. That one morning I would wake up, dread the day, fear being awake inside my skin, and when my autopilot kicks in with 'Just one cup of coffee—then you can return,' that I would say to myself, 'LIAR!' I've been lying to myself for years—okay, decades. Sometimes I do even reply with 'liar,' but it still works. I get the coffee.

What I would rather tell you is that I have found some advanced system to create recovery for myself. I would rather reveal to you how I changed my life to healthy living, engaged myself in life-giving relationships, and began my community service. And the fact is, I did and I do. There are many healthy skills I have. Many of which I have actually figured out how to get myself to do repeatedly, and my life *has* changed because of it.

But some days, it's just the coffee. All the healthy life skills in the world could not get me out of bed, but lowering my expectations and placing no demands (well, only one, simple, desirable request) on me works. And it works 99% of the time. And as the days have gone by and added up, each simple, doable, seemingly low expectation has added up to quite a rich life if I think about it.

There are people who would say I have made a difference for them. My kindness, sometimes even my crassness, has impacted them in a positive way. And they have gotten up and their days have added up and love has spread once again. I bet it's the same with you. I bet there are people who would say that your seemingly small acts of love have paid huge dividends. You cooked a meal, sent a card, made a call, stopped to visit, and the love you showed was imperative to that person's life.

So, today, the challenge—'just one'...just one act of love. Then, maybe, a few minutes later, when that one is done, you can lie to yourself again and say 'Just one more.' No telling what might happen by the end of the day."

You see, you can will yourself into making certain choices; you don't have to wait until your emotions subside. **Positive feelings follow positive action.** You don't have to wait until you stop feeling anxious about the messy house to take the kids to the beach. You can still choose to practice certain behaviors even if they're uncomfortable or scary—just do it afraid. Maybe you're new at your workplace and you're the shy, silent type. You love connecting with people and having deep one-on-one conversation, but in order to

> *Positive feelings follow positive action.*

get that, you will have to climb out of your comfort zone and actually initiate contact with your coworkers. The thought of making new friends might be a scary one for you, but you make a rule for yourself that you will make three contacts at work every day—you will strike up three conversations—and then you can retreat to your desk and concentrate on work. After a while, you start getting to know people, and you realize, "This isn't so scary, I can do this!"

There is one category of self-care that I recommend for everyone, and it usually falls into the social or spiritual category. It's kind of weird because it doesn't seem to involve the self at all, yet it's so fulfilling. While each of us may do this a little differently, I have found it to be an unbelievable remedy for all of us. **I have had clients and friends who, after beginning to volunteer somewhere to help others, transformed their entire lives.** When the busyness of life and our own responsibilities overwhelm us, sometimes escaping it all to focus on a much bigger picture is exactly what we need. It's amazing what happens to us when we start to invest in the lives of others. Whether you mentor kids and teens or help stock at a local food pantry, helping others pays amazing dividends. Stephanie Licata blogged about how it changed her life:

"If you told me twenty years ago I would spend a big chunk of my time encouraging young women to serve people in need, I would have seriously laughed in your face.

The summer after senior year, I finally decided to join some of my friends on their youth trip to the Appalachian Mountains. Over 60 teens crammed into vans and drove through the night to reach our middle of nowhere spot. I had never seen anything like what I saw on our trip. There was a main drag with a Wal-Mart, Burger King, and all the regular stores from home. Make a small turn off this road and you witnessed extreme poverty. Young girls with multiple children and homes without running water were commonplace.

I was assigned to the outreach team. We traveled through the Appalachian Mountains giving out basic necessities to people in need. We were directed to a certain place that was referred to as 'the hole.' This was a muddy field with about 20 trailer homes, most of which had no refrigeration, running water, or a real bathroom. It would be the site of a life defining moment for me. At 18, I had never been concerned for people other than my immediate family or friends. Poverty was staring me straight in the face and there was no turning back.

The children at 'the hole' stole our hearts. They were so thankful for a loaf of bread, milk, and some new clothes. We quickly bonded with them and went back each day to visit, often bringing more clothes and food. On our last day, a little girl named Jennifer tugged on my shirt and asked for a dress. I pulled one out of the bag and she began to cry. "I will get it dirty," she said. Jennifer had no bathtub or shower in her trailer. At four years old, the simple joy of feeling clean was out of reach. We took her down to a nearby creek and helped wash away some of the dirt on her arms and legs. Embracing her new dress, Jennifer's eyes were filled with joy as she ran around in her new outfit.

This may seem like a simple silly moment, but it changed my life. I could never again pretend to live in my suburban bubble of self-ishness. I truly believe this experience defined the woman I was to become.[23]"

While sometimes self-care does require a little—or even a lot—of effort, it's always worth it in the end. For the sake of your relationships, **don't retreat, don't resign yourself, but restore. If you're going to give love to others, you have to fill up first.**

HOW TO APPLY THIS TO YOUR LIFE:

It's time to give yourself an honest self-assessment. How well are you taking care of yourself? You can't give your best at work, at home, or in relation-ships when you're running on empty. Step back and take a good look at your life in the four main areas: physical, emotional, mental, and spiritual If you were to give yourself a grade in each of those areas, what would you give yourself? Assign yourself a grade, and be honest. **What grade would you give in each area: physical -___, emotional - ___, mental - ___, and spiritual - ___?**

For each area that you listed and graded, list three things that you will make into a new habit in order to fill yourself. Some examples are: ex-ercise three times a week, have coffee with your best friend once a month, journal every Sunday, play some basketball with the guys after work, attend church with your kids, listen to your favorite music in the morning, etc.

Now for the key: volunteering. **What aspect of volunteering most appeals to you?** Is it serving a certain group: children, the elderly, the disabled, unwed mothers, minority groups, or animals? Is it a certain cause: poverty, hunger, abuse, or drug prevention? Is it a certain organization? This is the one step in the book that I think people will be less inclined to do even though the rewards are so great. Volunteering actually does feel foreign and backward to some people. But even if you are shy or introverted, I know many like you who have volunteered to stock shelves at a food pantry, sort clothes at a thrift shop, or do administrative tasks, and have felt deep rewards knowing that they have impacted the life of a child or a hurting family. I also know busy executives who volunteer once a month and are allowed to rearrange their volunteer time around their schedule. No matter who you are, give it a try, and you'll be so glad you did!

Now list three places you could volunteer. Underline the first place you will go for a tour.

Some places will let you try out volunteering without requiring a commitment. **When will you give it a try?**

Epilogue: Scheduled Sex

"You haven't had real sex until there are two dogs at the end of your bed staring at you." Bill Engvall

"So, when is the last time you had sex?" the therapist asked. This is a common question asked in marriage counseling. Unfortunately, he had a common answer as well: "It's been so long; I don't remember."

After breaking the ice, the couple talked about how hot and heavy their sex life had been early on. But then college kept her busy, his promotion called for more hours at work, and, eventually, the kids came. They never planned on not having sex; it just happened. She was always too tired. He got tired of asking.

In his video series, *Laugh Your Way to a Better Marriage*, Mark Gungor draws a very simple diagram to illustrate a very important concept. He draws a heart, representing a woman's emotion, then a smiley face representing her private parts. He explains that **if a man touches a woman's heart, then she'll let him touch her "happy place." Likewise, if a woman touches a man's "happy place," she will be allowed to touch his heart**. Mark explains how this reciprocal relationship creates a certain flow in our relationships, but we often go against the flow because we don't understand it. We discount sex like it is no big deal: it shouldn't be important—that's not what relationships are about. And this is where we fail our marriages. Mark explains:

> *...if a man touches a woman's heart, then she'll let him touch her "happy place." Likewise, if a woman touches a man's "happy place," she will be allowed to touch his heart.*

"The key to you getting what you want is giving your spouse what they want. And it is the perfect standoff. It is the ultimate standoff. It's not easy. You've got to constantly work for this. You can't disregard this. Some guys don't pay attention to the girl; they're never nice to the girl and wonder how come they never get any sex. Be nice to the girl—you've got to touch her heart. That's your key. You're blowing it. Girls, same thing with you."

Sex is kind of like a newborn baby. You have this precious, beautiful newborn baby, and you never in your life realized what it could feel like. There's this powerful connection that occurs. And this is how sex can be in marriage: a precious, beautiful experience that creates a powerful connection.

But when it's 6:00 in the morning, and you were already up at 2:00 and 3:00 and 4:00 and 4:15 and 4:30, it's just a little less precious, isn't it? But you still choose to care for the baby. Sex is like that too. Sometimes you are not in the mood—you are tired and uninterested—but you can still provide a much needed gift to your spouse. Yes, sex can be amazing (or you can make it amazing, even if it hasn't been yet), but nothing is great and spectacular and amazing every time, all the time.

Even when you're not in the mood to feed the baby, you still don't leave it to cry for days without food. You do what you need to do to take care of him. We can do the same with our spouses. Frankly, ladies, this doesn't have to last any longer than you want it to last. We have ways of moving things along so that sex doesn't have to take a lot of time when we are out of energy. We can choose whether we want a two-hour event or just a few minutes.

There are times when sex is supposed to be precious, amazing, and wonderful. And there are times when we can simply help meet a biological need to expel sperm. He is going to expel that sperm regularly, usually every 48-72 hours, depending on age, and you should be a part of that process. Touching a man's heart through sex has a strong biological component that strengthens the relationship. When men have an orgasm with a mate, they release a hormone that exists in another important other relationship. It exists when a woman nurses a child. A bonding hormone is released that literally creates a more loving, intimate relationship. A lot of women are missing out on this with their husbands because they don't realize the important part sexual intercourse plays in relational bonding. It's not just testosterone driving a man to release; he wants to be with you. He may not realize or understand it, but the bonding hormone drives him to be close to you in this way, and this is only achieved with an orgasm. Frankly, the impact of an orgasm on a human, man or woman, has far-reaching, positive effects. The hormones that occur in our bodies create such a cleansing and healing experience for us. We need to have more sex!

I've heard that the average couple has sex once a week. But I'm guessing most men would be more satisfied at a rate of two to three times a week. Remember the days when you were doing it two or three times a day? Somehow you made time then. But with work, kids, and all the responsibilities of life, sex often slips away from us over time. Whatever regular rate works out best for your life, it is imperative that it doesn't get pushed aside as a non-issue. Because this happens so often, I recommend couples have scheduled sex. No, it's not very Hollywood—but that's not real sex anyway. When couples come into my office, I ask them when they last had sex. Sometimes the answer is a few months, sometimes three years, sometimes eight years. I don't think people go into it thinking that they're not going to have sex for the next few years. No, it happens because a week passes and another week passes and then a month passes, until time gets away from us. Most women have no drive, so they don't initiate; the man has been rejected over and over, so he doesn't try anymore. Then it just becomes awkward. As comedian Bill Engvall says, "Women are like camels: they can go for months without drinking from the well." And it's true. Because women are biologically wired differently, refraining from sex is not an issue (except for that spurt in our thirties when we get a lot of hormones!). This is part of the problem. There are other challenges as well.

Another part of the problem is that **many men and women are not aware of the fact that most women do not have an orgasm through intercourse**. Most women need direct stimulation of the clitoris, and intercourse alone usually does not provide enough. Another factor is that women have a monthly cycle that interferes with good sex because of constantly changing hormone levels. So what worked last week to achieve an orgasm might not work this week. Simple friction leads to an orgasm for most men, most of the time. But for women, it can sometimes be a moving target. Some women do have a simple process, but most of us have to figure out how it works, and everyone is constantly learning. Men, if you can take instructions, especially as things change with our cycle, and respond with, "Whatever you say, baby," then she can help you in this process. If you are open enough in your relationship to communicate what you like and don't like, and to be patient and stay engaged when the process is difficult, sex can be satisfying for everyone.

...many men and women are not aware of the fact that most women do not have an orgasm through intercourse.

Sex doesn't have to be a big deal. However, I am sensitive to the fact that some of us have more complicated issues. I've worked with survivors rape and sexual abuse. There are issues that arise from these and other negative experiences. But these issues can still be worked out. Maybe you need help in this area.

There are a number of resources that exist to provide this help, like licensed sex therapists (and even faith-based sex therapists, if you are religious). The question is not "if" we should be having sex, but "how." How do we make this a good and wonderful part of our marriage? This is an important key to a happy, healthy relationship. It's not an "if" it works out. It's "when." You can't let time continue to pass by because sex is such a crucial part of marriage.

One of the greatest analogies I ever heard was when someone asked me what condition a relationship would be in if the two people had not spoken for 30 days—or even years. Most people know how dead and lifeless any relationship would be if the two people never spoke. As women, conversation is fulfilling for us. We like to talk and share our lives, our hopes, our dreams, and our struggles. We cannot imagine a relationship without talking for a month, let alone for years. Yet we seem to have no problem refraining from sex for months or years, though men tend to connect physically. What a sobering thought. **We have no idea just how dead and lifeless a marriage can become without this healthy way of connecting; the same as it would be if he didn't speak to you, not even a word, for years.** Sex is absolutely vital to the life and health of your marriage.

> *We have no idea just how dead and lifeless a marriage can become without this healthy way of connecting; the same as it would be if he didn't speak to you, not even a word, for years.*

HOW TO APPLY THIS TO YOUR LIFE:

Maybe this whole concept of having sex again after so long terrifies you. Maybe you don't think you can make that move anymore. Maybe you're so angry or dejected because it's been so long that you don't think it's really worth the effort to even try. If you're there, hang in there.

If you are a survivor, who has faced a traumatic event, what can you do to move forward in this area? If you need counseling who can you contact? Keep in mind that many latch on to the idea that sex is no big deal and will reduce your anxiety by telling you not to worry about it. Despite your history, make it your goal to determine "how" to make this happen, not "if" - **what can you do to move forward in this area?**

If marital conflict has separated you, love has died or time has passed, bite the bullet and move on to the next question.

This week you are going to start meeting that need of your spouse. So guys – it's time to start letting your wife talk about her day, listen, show empathy, laugh with her, hold her. And gals – yes, it's time to get a little physical with your hubby. Touch him – every time you cross paths. And I don't mean trying to wipe a stain off his shirt – I mean touch his chest, arms, face . . . and his happy place. Time to be purposeful - Because saying you're going to do it and doing it are two different things. So what's your plan guys? Gals? **Write out here what you will intentionally do this week to meet the need of your spouse.** Include days, times, and what you will be doing.

So now you have your plan in place . . . time to rise to the occasion. Be bold. Remember – you used to do this stuff all of the time! AND if your spouse doesn't notice or "get" the new attention at first – it's ok! Keep working at it.

When will you be having sex this week? What day? What time? **What is the *best* way to make this happen** (consider what's good for your spouse!)? Guys – is it after your wife's favorite meal, show, and a hot shower? Gals – is it a 5 minute quickie in the morning right before he checks his email? What works for him? What works for her?

And one last thing – Orgasms . . . ahhhh, orgasms. Guys – remember to follow her lead; Gals – remember to actually give some lead to follow. Lastly – HAVE FUN! **Gals – write down what turns you on**. How do you like to be touched? Where do you like to be touched? Lights on? Lights off? Bed or counter? **Guys – write down what turns you on.** How do you like to be touched? Where do you like to be touched? Lights on? Lights off? Bed or counter?

How will you communicate this *effectively?* Perhaps demanding may not be the appropriate approach – maybe it's a whisper in the ear during foreplay. Maybe it's a sit-down discussion on a date. Maybe you write it down and slip your spouse a note in his briefcase; her purse. **Write out your plan to effectively communicate what you like.** Remember be specific about the time, day, and all the details you need to make it happen!

Endnotes

1 Covey, Stephen R. *First Things First*. New York: Simon and Shuster, 2001.

2 Cloud, Henry and John Townsend. *Boundaries in Marriage*. Grand Rapids: Zondervan, 2002.

3 *Ibid.*

4 Killoran, Maureen. "Q-Tip It." Spiritquest.ws 2004. Web. 01 June 2012

5 Roosevelt, Eleanor. *This is My Story*. New York: Garden City Publishing, 1937.

6 Duchovny, David. BrainyQuote.com. Xplore Inc, 2013. Web. 11 February 2013.

7 Smalley, Gary and John Trent. *The Two Sides of Love*. Carol Stream: Tyndale House, 1990.

8 Patterson, Kerry, et al. *Crucial Conversations: Tools for Talking When Stakes Are High*. New York: McGraw-Hill, 2002.

9 Smalley, Gary, et al. *The DNA of Relationships*. Carol Stream: Tyndale House, 2004.

10 Smalley, Gary, et.al. *The DNA of Relationships for Couples*. Carol Stream: Tyndale House, 2004.

11 Roser, Mark. "Walking the Forgiveness Path" New and Improved. The Innovative Brain Newsletter, 2007. Web. 8 Feb. 2013

12 *Ibid.*

13 *Ibid.*

14 Harley, Willard F. *His Needs, Her Needs*. Grand Rapids: Revell, 1986. Print.

15 Cousins, Norman. *Head First: The Biology of Hope and the Healing Power of the Human Spirit*. New York: Penguin Books, 1990.

16 Smalley, Gary, et al. *The DNA of Relationships*. Carol Stream: Tyndale House, 2004.

17 Collins, Jim. *Good to Great*. New York: HarperCollins, 2001.

18 *Ibid.*

20 Terkeurst, Lysa. "The Package Deal" Proverbs 31 Ministries Radio. Proverbs 31 Ministries, 22 May 2012. Web. 9 Feb. 2013

21 Parrot, Les and Leslie. *When Bad Things Happen to Good Marriages: How to Stay Together When Life Pulls You Apart.* Grand Rapids: Zondervan, 2001.

22 Deschene, Lori. (Stevenson, Cat Li) "What it Really Means to Take Care of Yourself" Tiny Buddha. Tiny Buddha, 3 May 2011. Web. 8 Feb. 2013

23 Simmons, Rachel. (Licata, Stephanie) "How Volunteering as a Teen Changed My Life" Rachel Simmons. Rachel Simmons, 21 July 2010. Web. 8 Feb. 2013

www.ingramcontent.com/pod-product-compliance
Lightning Source LLC
Chambersburg PA
CBHW070020300526
45794CB00001B/371